Laura Kalbag

ACCESSIBILITY FOR EVERYONE

MORE FROM A BOOK APART

Practical Design Discovery
Dan Brown

Demystifying Public Speaking
Lara Hogan

JavaScript for Web Designers
Mat Marquis

Practical SVG
Chris Coyier

Design for Real Life
Eric Meyer & Sara Wachter-Boettcher

Git for Humans
David Demaree

Going Responsive
Karen McGrane

Responsive Design: Patterns & Principles
Ethan Marcotte

Designing for Touch
Josh Clark

Responsible Responsive Design
Scott Jehl

Visit abookapart.com for our full list of titles.

Publisher: Jeffrey Zeldman
Designer: Jason Santa Maria
Executive Director: Katel LeDû
Developmental Editors: Erin Kissane, Caren Litherland
Line Editor: Lisa Maria Martin
Technical Editor: Léonie Watson
Copyeditor: Kate Towsey
Proofreader: Katel LeDû
Book Producer: Ron Bilodeau

ISBN: 978-1-937557-61-4

A Book Apart
New York, New York
http://abookapart.com

10 9 8 7 6 5 4 3 2 1

TABLE OF CONTENTS

FOREWORD

FIRST, I'D LIKE TO applaud you for buying, or borrowing, a book on web accessibility—not because learning about accessibility is something you *should* do, but because you're stepping out of your comfort zone. Learning a new tool or framework is one thing, but rethinking who you are creating things *for* is quite another. It means accepting that you might have failed people in the past, and that's equally challenging.

I'm also glad you chose this particular book. In less capable hands, writing about accessibility paints it as complex, tedious, and scary. While there are many technical challenges to face—which Laura deftly addresses here—the most important lesson is that *everyone* uses the web quite differently. And that's whether or not they have what you may consider disabilities.

It's a big deal, but don't worry. Laura's book teaches you how to navigate accessibility, how to develop strategies for it, and how to embrace it as a fresh challenge. With practice, designing and building inclusive interfaces will become second nature. You won't work any harder, you'll just do better work—and better serve a more diverse group of people.

—Heydon Pickering

For Suzy and Judy

1
CONSIDERING ACCESSIBILITY

THE BBC HOMEPAGE is a brilliant example of accessible web practices in the wild (**FIG 1.1**). The layout clearly distinguishes the different areas of content. The simple interactive elements are easy to use. The copy is understandable—helped along by readable typography and a high contrast between the text and background colors. And the page is straightforward to navigate for people using a screen reader and keyboard navigation.

Crucially, the BBC homepage is also a team effort. The accessibility of the site isn't just the responsibility of one lone developer who fixed all the problems before the page went live. Product managers, content strategists, and information architects defined the homepage's content and structure based on information and goals provided by researchers and executives. Copywriters and journalists wrote the clear and easy-to-understand copy. The team's designers shaped the central content's simple interactive behavior, selected accessible colors, and chose readable typography. The developers built in screen reader accessibility and keyboard navigation support.

Every decision a team makes affects a site's accessibility. Just like content, interaction design, or web performance, accessibil-

FIG 1.1: The BBC homepage requires a very flexible design as the news content is updated so regularly and can be customized by users. The background can even be themed to fit news events.

ity is a core consideration of creating websites. And—contrary to what many teams assume—it can't be addressed separately from the rest of the website creation process.

In fact, if you work on the web in any capacity, accessibility is your job.

EXCUSES, EXCUSES

Not convinced that accessibility considerations belong in every part of the design and development process? Many people aren't—often because of a few widely held misconceptions. If you've been avoiding accessibility in your web work, some of these excuses may sound familiar:

- "Accessibility is boring." In the web industry, we tend to obsess over tools. We always want to know about the coolest new framework or the shiniest new aesthetic trend. These are avoidance tactics. While our tools can be cool, we're distracting ourselves from what really matters: why our products exist and who benefits from them.

- **"We can't tell if anyone really benefits."** There's a common misconception that people with disabilities don't use the internet, something I'll address in greater detail in Chapter 2. For now, I'll just say that it's a load of nonsense. At any rate, accessibility doesn't just benefit people with specific disabilities, it improves the usability of a website for *everyone*.
- **"We don't know what to do!"** That's precisely why this book exists. You'll discover that there are many ways to approach accessibility. A few small changes can make a big difference. Or you can build an accessible site from the start, creating a fantastic experience for a wide audience from the very beginning.
- **"It's too hard and there's too much to do."** Working in design and technology, we do challenging work every day. The web is always moving and changing, and so we frequently come across complications and bugs when we're building sites. We don't normally give up at the first sign of an issue; we find a way around it, without compromising the experience. The same is true of accessibility; we just need to add new techniques to our toolkit.

Can we agree to stop making these excuses? Accessibility is a win-win situation for all involved. It's even good for business: by making our sites accessible for everyone, we also increase our potential user base.

But let's not get ahead of ourselves. First we need to understand what accessibility really means.

INCLUSION

I'll start with some definitions. *Accessibility* in the physical world is the degree to which an environment is usable by as many people as possible. *Web accessibility* is the degree to which a website is usable by as many people as possible. We can think about both kinds of accessibility as forms of *inclusion*.

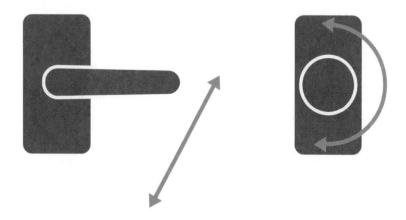

FIG 1.2: Pivoting handles (left) only require a gentle push from above. Spherical door knobs (right) require a gripped, twisting motion. (Pivoting handles are so easy to use, my dog can use them. Though I really wish he couldn't!)

In our physical spaces, we understand that accessibility isn't just about wheelchairs—our environments are designed to accommodate an increasingly wide range of needs. For example, interior designers are phasing out spherical door knobs in favor of pivoting door handles, because pivoting handles make it easier for people with limited movement in their arms and hands to open doors (**FIG 1.2**).

Similarly, many pedestrian traffic crossings play a tone to let people with visual difficulties know that it's safe to cross. Movies offer subtitles so that people with hearing difficulties can follow the dialogue. And signage is written with as few words as possible to help people with reading difficulties understand their environment. These design features don't make the objects less usable for those *without* the particular impairments they address—in fact, they usually make a product easier for everyone to use.

Product designers and architects often pay great attention to the accessibility of objects and spaces. They understand that an object designed inclusively can be used by more people and thus have wider commercial appeal. In many countries, public spaces must be inclusive by law: excluding a person by way of design from a non-accessible public space is discriminatory and therefore illegal. However, most laws haven't yet caught up to the new medium that is the web. Laws vary from country to country and those that do apply to the web are not always enforced.

Universal design

Universal design is a concept coined by architect Ronald L. Mace, founder of the Center for Universal Design. After contracting polio at age nine, Mace used a wheelchair for most of his life. He had to be carried up and down stairs to attend classes, and his wheelchair didn't fit through the doors of public restrooms. Mace's experiences led him to study architecture, and later specialize in accessibility. He considered universal design an evolution of accessible design:

> *Universal design is the design of products and environments to be usable by all people, to the greatest extent possible, without the need for adaptation or specialized design.*

The distinction between universal and accessible design is subtle but important. *Accessible design* considers the needs of people with disabilities. So, for example, accessible design might result in a building having a wheelchair ramp attached to its far side, as an afterthought. It might not be convenient for people using wheelchairs, and it's unlikely to be used by people who find it faster to use the stairs, but at least there's some form of access (**FIG 1.3**).

On the other hand, universal design considers the needs of a diverse human population. Universal design might result in a building with a combined ramp and stairs, opening access to all and forcing no one to go out of their way to choose one option or the other (**FIG 1.4**).

FIG 1.3: This zigzagging wheelchair ramp installed over a steep garden is an extreme example of bolt-on ugliness and poor design.

FIG 1.4: This ramp could be used just as easily by cyclists or parents pushing strollers as by people using wheelchairs. It doesn't look out of place. In fact, it contributes to the architecture.

FIG 1.5: The New York Times's website enables readers to change the body text size. But the text size buttons are hidden in a menu at the top of the page. You can't see the text being resized without scrolling down.

Whereas accessible design creates products that are usable by those with disabilities, universal design creates products for the widest possible audience, which includes, but isn't limited to, people with disabilities. Good universal architectural design is elegant, considerate of all its users, and seems to effortlessly suit the space.

This contrast in approach is directly transferable to web design. Accessible web design might mean adding a button to your site that allows people to view the text at a larger size. It's yet another element crowding a page layout, and people have to go out of their way to find it (**FIG 1.5**).

Universal web design, applied to the same problem, might mean making *all* the text larger so that a greater number of people can read the text without needing to find a button or use zoom shortcuts (**FIG 1.6**).

Throughout this book, I take *a universal design approach to accessibility* wherever possible. Universal web accessibility helps us create sites that are usable by the widest, most diverse audience, rather than creating bolt-on solutions that might benefit one group at the expense of another. (But I won't always use the terms "universal design" or "universal web accessibility" because they're a bit of a mouthful.)

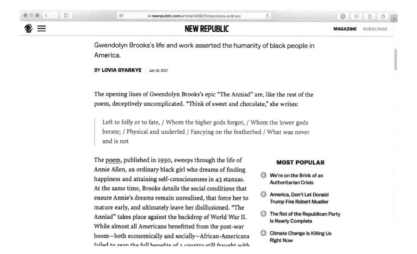

Gwendolyn Brooks's life and work asserted the humanity of black people in America.

BY LOVIA GYARKYE | July 10, 2017

The opening lines of Gwendolyn Brooks's epic "The Anniad" are, like the rest of the poem, deceptively uncomplicated. "Think of sweet and chocolate," she writes:

Left to folly or to fate, / Whom the higher gods forgot, / Whom the lower gods berate; / Physical and underfed / Fancying on the featherbed / What was never and is not

The poem, published in 1950, sweeps through the life of Annie Allen, an ordinary black girl who dreams of finding happiness and attaining self-consciousness in 43 stanzas. At the same time, Brooks details the social conditions that ensure Annie's dreams remain unrealized, that force her to mature early, and ultimately leave her disillusioned. "The Anniad" takes place against the backdrop of World War II. While almost all Americans benefitted from the post-war boom—both economically and socially—African-Americans failed to reap the full benefits of a country still fraught with

MOST POPULAR

1. We're on the Brink of an Authoritarian Crisis
2. America, Don't Let Donald Trump Fire Robert Mueller
3. The Rot of the Republican Party Is Nearly Complete
4. Climate Change Is Killing Us Right Now

FIG 1.6: The default body text size on the New Republic's site is a generous 20 pixels, which makes the page instantly more inviting as it's easy to read.

EMPATHY

Empathy is the ability to share the feelings of others. It's what makes us good at creating products for other people as we can better understand their problems and create solutions that fit their needs. It's always easier to create products for people who have the same needs as us, since we understand our own requirements—and the reasons behind them—better than anybody else. Many successful products are created when people "scratch their own itch."

The problem with creating products to suit only our needs is that, in the tech industry, we are largely people of similar ages, abilities, backgrounds, and educational and financial statuses. We end up creating products for people just like us, forgetting that other people may have requirements that differ from, or even conflict with, our own. To create more useful, usable products, we need to understand and care about differing needs.

When Jen Simmons interviewed Dale Cruse for *The Web Ahead* podcast (http://bkaprt.com/afe/01-01/), Cruse suggested that the average accessibility professional is older than the average web professional, perhaps because many people gain empathy through age. As we get older, we start to experience age-related impairments, such as eyesight degeneration or motor difficulties associated with conditions like arthritis. If your eyesight is poor, or you struggle to use a keyboard and mouse comfortably for long periods of time, it's much easier to understand and empathize with others experiencing similar problems.

Empathy in design is far easier when we work in diverse teams. Diversity comes from a range of ages, abilities, ethnicities, socio-economic classes, personal backgrounds, genders, education levels, and many more characteristics which give each of us a unique experience of the world. Spending meaningful time with people whose experiences differ from our own can help us develop a greater understanding of each other's needs. The greater capacity a team has for understanding their audience, the more likely they are to solve that audience's problems.

Having a diverse team can also prevent us from "othering" our audience. Have you ever heard someone refer to users or clients as "stupid"? It's easy to be dismissive of the people using our products if we think in us-versus-them terms. This is also why some designers want to avoid the term "user" in favor of "person" or "human." Alternative terms can be a little tricky, so while I use "user" throughout this book, it's important to remember the essential humanity of everyone interacting with our products and interfaces.

Believing we know what's best for others, despite our differing needs, can also result in a patronizing and incorrect solution (sometimes referred to as "colonial design"). For example, sometimes when developers first learn about screen readers, they provide additional instructions and cues in text that only visible to screen readers. They're trying to be helpful, but these additional instructions on how to use the interface are usually unnecessary, disruptive and distracting for people who just want to get to the page content.

SCREEN READERS

Screen readers have become the symbol for web accessibility, and understandably so: as a piece of assistive technology that reads the contents of a screen (either aloud via audio output or via a braille output device), screen readers have made text-based webpages accessible for those with visual impairments.

Screen readers used to be very expensive, specialist software that few people could afford. Job Access With Speech (JAWS), a Windows-based screen reader, has been around since 1995 and is probably the most capable and well-known screen reader of its kind. But JAWS currently costs around $900, which could be prohibitively expensive for many people.

Apple's VoiceOver screen reader has been revolutionary for users of Apple computers and devices. Before Mac OS X 10.4 introduced this feature, screen readers were usually stand-alone software that could be installed on a computer. VoiceOver, however, included a screen reader as a core part of the operating system and on every device (although, granted, they are expensive devices). It works with all Apple software, including the browser, and works with all native controls provided to developers on the Apple platform.

Over the last few years, free and open-source screen readers have popped up, such as NVDA (NonVisual Desktop Access) for Windows, Linux Screen Reader (LSR), and Orca for Linux. Window-Eyes, a proprietary screen reader for Windows, used to be as expensive as JAWS but is now free. Microsoft has a screen reader called Narrator which is similar to Apple's VoiceOver and has recently been improved a great deal. Both VoiceOver and Narrator can be enabled quickly, providing instant access to anyone requiring a screen reader. No configuration is needed unless a user has other preferences (FIG 1.7).

When deciding on which screen reader you want to use (or can afford), you're left with striking a balance. JAWS *is* expensive, but it offers better support for more applications across Windows than other screen readers. VoiceOver has good support on Apple's own apps and web browsers, but mixed support across other developers' apps.

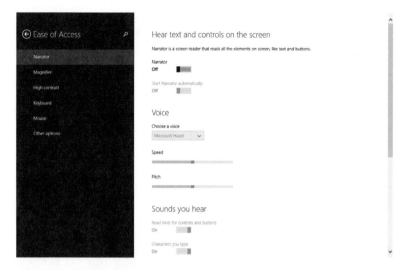

FIG 1.7: Narrator Settings in Windows 8.1: Narrator also has a developer mode that helps you identify which objects are accessible to Narrator (http://bkaprt.com/afe/01-02/).

Screen readers don't just benefit those with visual impairments. Some people can consume information more comfortably and conveniently by hearing text rather than reading it. For example, many people prefer audiobooks over reading, and sighted users with learning difficulties may prefer screen readers for reading lengthy amounts of text aloud.

Screen readers also enable people to engage in other activities while listening—such as driving while listening to an SMS text message. As the web starts finding its way into more mobile systems, we're likely to come across more use cases like this.

For people with visual impairments, a refreshable braille display can be used with a screen reader. Some braille displays also enable users to write in braille and have their input automatically translated back into text (**FIG 1.8**).

Keyboard navigation

Keyboard navigation describes a situation when a person uses only a keyboard to access a computer or site. Screen readers are often (but not always!) paired with keyboard navigation.

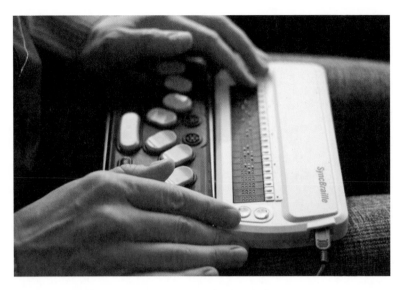

FIG 1.8: Braille displays are very expensive, which limits how many people can afford to use them. (Photo courtesy of Karola Riegler http://bkaprt.com/afe/01-03/).

Sometimes specialist keyboards, such as custom keyboards or on-screen keyboards, are used to assist with keyboard use and keyboard-only navigation.

Most keyboard-based web browsing uses the Up and Down cursor keys for scrolling, the Tab key for moving between interactive elements, and the Space bar or Enter key for interaction. Screen readers will often map keys to different, more contextually relevant, commands.

Keyboard navigation isn't just used by screen reader users, it's also very valuable for those who don't have a mouse or have difficulties using a mouse. Lots of programmers favor keyboard navigation because they spend so much time in text-based console windows. And many people use keyboard navigation when filling out forms on the web—you may not even realize how often you tab between fields!

BEYOND SCREEN READERS

In the same way that accessibility in our physical environment isn't just about wheelchairs, accessibility on the web isn't just about screen readers. People in diverse environments and with varying abilities benefit from well-considered accessibility.

For every device, there are many different ways to input and output information from a computer and the web. Assistive technology is just another bridge between the user and their device. Some inputs, such as the standard mouse and hardware keyboard, are familiar to anyone using a desktop computer. But people use alternatives for a multitude of reasons.

Navigation hardware

There are many alternatives to mice and cursor-based navigation: touchpads and touchscreens, upright or vertical mice, trackball or rollerball mice, even foot-operated mice.

The behavior of these alternatives is generally the same or similar to hand-operated mouse behavior, and requires little additional software. There are also alternatives to mice that require some extra configuration to fit an individual user's preferences, such as switch inputs and eye trackers.

Switch inputs

Switch devices allow people to interact with a screen via a switch. The switch's software moves through options on the screen, and people trigger the switch when their desired option is highlighted. Switch inputs combine hardware and software, and may be mechanical buttons, adjustable pressure switches, foot plates, handlebar-like grasp switches, or electronic sensors. They can be used to replace keyboards, mice, or both.

Apple recently made their operating systems natively accessible to switch control, which means you can easily test the general switch accessibility of your sites on iOS and macOS. Mac's Switch Control can be enabled from the Accessibility settings, which house a huge variety of customizable settings. iOS and Mac-compatible switches are available to buy from specialty stores (some are Bluetooth-enabled, which is handy for the iPhone!). But if you don't have a physical switch, you can still use touch or mouse clicks to trigger interactions.

Eye trackers

Eye trackers are similar to electronic or sensor switches, but rely on a camera to analyze the movement of the user's eyes and navigate the screen accordingly. Eye trackers can be used to help people with disabilities communicate via a computer, but they are generally very expensive.

Dwell Control was also recently added to macOS to enable the use of eye-tracking or head-tracking to control the mouse. The Dwell Control Home Panel helps users click, drag, and scroll to interact with the screen (**FIG 1.9**).

Speech recognition

Speech recognition software is used with a microphone so that a computer can be operated with spoken commands. Since speech recognition technology has improved so much in recent years, it's something that many of us are familiar with from our smartphones. Apple has Siri, Microsoft has Cortana, and Google has Google Assistant.

These simple virtual assistants can work with any voice, though they generally aren't as capable as dedicated voice-user interfaces or speech-to-text software. The more advanced, expensive software is often "trained" to a user's voice by having them read from a set text. This enables the software to recognize nuances and accents in the user's speech and improve its accuracy.

Screen magnifiers

Screen magnifiers offer zooming functionality and are built into operating systems like macOS, Windows, and Linux. Screen magnifiers usually have two modes: the first involves magnifying a small area of the screen (directed by the cursor) as a picture-in-picture, while the second mode magnifies the entire screen, zooming in on a particular area. (**FIG 1.10**).

FIG 1.9: The user chooses an interaction from the Dwell Control Home Panel, and then hovers (or dwells) over the item they want to interact with. There is a countdown to ensure the correct item is selected.

FIG 1.10: Screen magnifier using picture-in-picture magnification (left), and the same desktop using full-screen magnification (right).

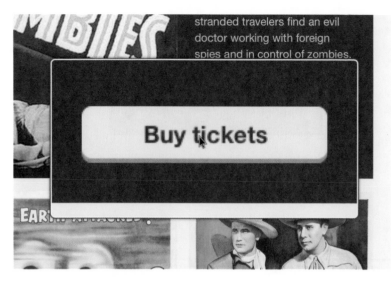

Fig 1.11: When an image is magnified, the text can become pixelated.

Though screen magnifier tools are useful when a page can't be zoomed in the browser, these tools tend to obscure or hide other content, reducing the readability of the whole screen. Images of text render poorly when zoomed, and should be avoided (for this and other reasons, which we'll look at in Chapter 5) (**FIG 1.11**).

Assistive technologies can give people access to the web who wouldn't otherwise have been able to engage. But they can only help people to a point. For example, video players can be made easier to access by using assistive technologies, but the video content can only be fully accessible for hearing-impaired people using subtitles or transcripts and, for visually-impaired people, using audio description.

Making our sites accessible starts with the understanding that people access the web differently, and continues with *every* member of the team ensuring their output is inclusive.

WE'RE IN THIS TOGETHER

When we start learning how to make our sites accessible, we can struggle because, well, accessibility itself isn't always accessible. Take *a11y*, for example. You might know what a11y means if you've heard of *i18n*—they're both alphanumeric acronyms. A11y stands for "accessibility" and *i18n* for "internationalization". The letters between the first and last have been replaced by a number representing the number of missing letters. Even I need to reread that sentence to understand it, and I'm the one who wrote it! It's definitely not universally accessible.

Along with the mystifying jargon, accessibility is often presented as something that should be left to "experts." We do need experts for their specialized knowledge and guidance, but there aren't enough accessibility experts in the world to leave the task of building an accessible web in their hands alone.

That's why it's up to us—you, me, designers and developers, writers and information architects, everyone—to make the web a fairer place.

2 DISABILITIES AND IMPAIRMENTS

" *Without the internet, I'd be stuck. I can't use books. I'd be sitting in the corner with a dunce's hat."*
—SAM

MEET SAM. He's my brother. In many ways, he's no different from so many people who happen to build websites: he's a college graduate in his late twenties; he loves music, sports, reading, video games, and movies; and he spends tons of time online.

But the internet isn't easy for Sam to use. He has to focus, concentrate, and be determined. Any task he undertakes will probably take two or three times the amount of time it would take me. Using the web isn't something Sam can do in five minutes with the TV on in the background; it's an all-or-nothing task. And since there's a limited amount of time in the day, he has to prioritize what he wants to do in that time. If a website forces him out of his comfort zone, it becomes a chore and won't be worthwhile.

Sam has cerebral palsy (CP), a neurological condition that mostly impacts muscle control and movement. CP affects 1 in 400 people, and is completely different from one person to another. Some people with CP are Paralympic footballers, while others with CP have very little muscle control and need to use a wheelchair to get around. Sam's CP is moderate to mild. He can walk unaided, but his balance can make it slow and precarious. His limited fine-motor control makes using mice and keyboards difficult. His body has constant small tremors and spasms, which means that any kind of physical input requires a lot of concentration.

And Sam has other impairments that, while not directly related to cerebral palsy, are common among those with CP. He's shortsighted, so he needs to wear glasses when he's reading from a screen. He also has dyslexia, which makes reading exhausting and makes it hard for him to concentrate for long periods at a time. The combined challenges in reading and typing make online communication hard work.

Despite these difficulties, Sam spends nine hours a day on the web. He loves research and fact-checking. The internet allows him to find out information on almost anything in the world. His brilliant memory leads him to combine and contextualize information unlike anyone else I know. In Chapter 1, I cited a common misconception that disabled people don't use the internet—and yet Sam couldn't do without it: "I can't imagine what life was like for disabled people before the internet. It allowed me to function in a mainstream educational environment."

DEFINING DISABILITY

An estimated 37,627,800 people in the US—12.1% of the population—have a disability. In the UK, 16% of working-age adults have a disability, amounting to over 11 million people. But what is a disability?

Disabilities is an umbrella term, covering impairments, activity limitations, and participation restrictions. An impairment is a problem in body function or structure; an activity limitation is a difficulty encountered by an individual in executing a task

or action; while a participation restriction is a problem experienced by an individual in involvement in life situations.
   —*World Health Organization*

That's a tricky description, because impairments are multilevel and spread across a spectrum—we are all physically abled in different ways, some more than others. If you wear glasses, you probably don't consider yourself disabled; but if your eyesight were to deteriorate by a few degrees, you may suddenly find yourself needing further assistance.

Individuals may also have more than one impairment, which alone don't cause much difficulty, but together can create a more significant disability. For example, age may cause your eyesight to deteriorate, forcing you to enlarge screen text size, while arthritis might leave you with impaired coordination, making a mouse awkward to use, particularly with accuracy and at speed. The combination would have quite an impact on your ability to use the internet.

"Disabled"

There are many nuances in the language around disability. In the US and UK, disability-rights groups tend to refer to a person as being "disabled": "Sam is disabled." However, many people have started using "has a disability" instead: "Sam has a disability." Using "disability" as a noun changes the focus: Sam *has* a disability, but he is not *defined by* that disability. Others with disabilities prefer the adjective "disabled" for the opposite reason: the world disables them when it forces them to interact in environments that aren't designed to consider their needs.

In this book, I talk about people who *have* disabilities, rather than people who *are* disabled. When we're designing for the web, thinking of the person *before* the disability helps us focus on universal design: we consider the needs of our diverse audience rather than create a false separation between "people without disabilities" and "people with disabilities."

TYPES OF DISABILITY

Five main areas of disability affect our use of the web: visual impairments, auditory impairments, motor impairments, cognitive impairments, and vestibular disorders and seizures.

Visual impairments

A huge spectrum of disabilities involves eyesight, and gives rise to a wide range of needs. Problems with eyesight aren't just focused on the function of our eyes, but also on how our brains perceive what our eyes see. Conditions such as nearsightedness, farsightedness, and astigmatism are very common in people of all ages and tend to worsen with age. Conditions can also vary from day to day, and throughout the day. Visual impairments affect everything we see on the web, and can benefit from considerate text sizes, typography, and layouts.

Color blindness

Color blindness is a common visual impairment that affects up to 8% of men and 0.5% of women. Color blindness doesn't mean that a person can't see any colors, or that they only see in grayscale, but that they cannot see a particular color or distinguish certain colors from one another.

Normal color vision uses all three light cones in our eyes, and is known as *trichromacy*. Each cone has a different sensitivity to light wavelengths—red, green, and blue. Deficiencies in different cones create different types of color blindness (**FIG 2.1**):

- *Deuteranopia* causes reds to look lighter, and makes them easily confused with greens.
- *Protanopia* is a rare red-cone deficiency that makes pinks appear blue, and makes dark reds and blacks easy to confuse.
- People with both deuteranopia and protanopia are known as *red-green color blind*. They have difficulty distinguishing between reds, greens, browns, and oranges, and may confuse blue and purple hues.

FIG 2.1: A kingfisher in its original photo, then duplicated (left to right) with simulated deuteranopia, protanopia, tritanopia and monochromacy. Photograph courtesy of Foundry (http://bkaprt.com/afe/02-01/).

- *Tritanopia* is an extremely rare blue-cone deficiency that causes people to confuse blue with green and yellow with violet.
- *Monochromacy* is the rarest type of color blindness, affecting just one person in 33,000. It's similar to seeing in grayscale. Affected people often wear dark glasses in normal light due to increased light sensitivity.

Color blindness has a significant impact on the readability and comprehension of a page. Text colors need to be readable against background colors, and because different people perceive color differently, it's unreliable to use color to signify meaning.

Eyesight loss

People with partial eyesight loss need clear labels, readable text sizes, and a high contrast between text and background colors. They may want to invert screen colors or hide background images to make a page easier to read. They may also use a screen reader or braille display, and will benefit from well-written HTML and a text alternative for images and video.

FIG 2.2: That kingfisher again, this time simulating (left to right) macular degeneration, glaucoma, and diabetic retinopathy.

- *Age-related macular degeneration* is the leading cause of blindness in adults. It causes the center of your field of vision—what you're looking at directly—to be blurry or obscured, making it hard to watch TV, look at photos, and read (**FIG 2.2**).
- *Glaucoma* is the result of damage to the optic nerve, and has the opposite effect of macular degeneration: the edges of your field of vision are obscured (**FIG 2.2**).
- *Diabetic retinopathy* occurs when diabetes damages the blood vessels in light-sensitive eye tissue. It causes dark spots in your field of vision, obscuring or distorting what you see (**FIG 2.2**).

Auditory impairments

Some people with auditory impairments are born with hearing loss, while others lose their hearing through age, illness, or accident.

- *Conductive hearing loss* occurs when sound can't get to the inner ear. It's usually caused by a blockage or abnormality in the ear. This type of hearing loss makes sounds quieter, but not usually distorted.
- *Sensorineural hearing loss* (sometimes referred to as sensory, cochlear, neural, or inner-ear hearing loss) is caused by damage to the nerves in the ear, distorting sound and making speech harder to understand.

Many people with hearing loss use written and spoken language to read and communicate, making the web a very valuable tool. Technologies such as email and instant messaging can be useful for communicating where face-to-face or telephone conversations are difficult. However, audio and video content can be inaccessible when alternative ways to view the content aren't provided.

People who are deaf sometimes use sign language, particularly if they've been profoundly deaf since birth. There's a common misperception that sign language is universal and that it neatly corresponds to spoken language. That's not the case. For example, American Sign Language (ASL) and British Sign Language (BSL) differ from each other much more than spoken US English and British English do.

Some people with hearing loss can lip-read, but this depends on the person they're watching. If someone has a different accent and therefore forms different lip shapes from those the lip-reader is used to, they can be harder to understand. Large mustaches and beards are also problematic. (That's a good reason to keep your fashionable facial hair trimmed!)

Motor impairments

An enormous range of conditions can cause motor impairments: cerebral palsy (as explained earlier in the chapter) affects muscle control and movement; neural-tube defects cause weakness, paralysis, and abnormal eye movement; muscle and joint conditions like muscular dystrophy, arthritis, and Ehlers-Danlos syndrome cause pain and difficulty moving. Traumatic injuries to the brain or spine can also cause a debilitating array of neurological, motor, sensory, and cognitive problems. And physical labor or repetitive movements (as you might find in computer-based jobs) can lead to repetitive strain injury, carpal tunnel syndrome, and other musculoskeletal disorders.

Motor impairments can make the use of standard inputs and outputs difficult. People may struggle to use a mouse, keyboard, or touchpad depending on their physical condition and motor control in their arms, hands, and fingers. Such challenges can also make handheld devices, like mobile phones, completely inoperable.

Interactions that require moving a mouse over a small area, selecting text, and right-clicking—such as filling out forms or using dropdown menus, navigation, and multimedia—can be difficult and time-consuming when small, controlled movements are hard to make. Motor impairments can also mean that user response time is slow: interfaces requiring interaction at a particular time, especially in games and animations, may result in missed cues.

As mentioned earlier, my brother Sam has limited fine-motor control in his hands. To limit typing, he uses speech-recognition software for writing emails and tweets. Sam often finds himself saying the same word over and over again, hoping that the software will pick up on what he's saying. The software often makes mistakes, which means he needs to say "scratch that" aloud to undo the last typed phrase. He's constantly frustrated that the software fails to recognize what he's saying. Speech-recognition software still has a long way to go before it can provide a flawless experience.

Cognitive impairments

Cognitive difficulties are incredibly diverse, and the way people interact with web content will vary depending on their condition. Cognitive issues that are particularly relevant to the web include:

- **Memory:** difficulties remembering the task one is trying to accomplish, or where one is within a site.
- **Attention:** difficulty focusing on large amounts of information, or any information for prolonged periods.
- **Problem-solving:** difficulty processing information, particularly if the content on the page is not what's expected.
- **Text processing:** difficulty understanding text, and difficulty expressing understanding through speech and language.
- **Math processing:** difficulty understanding mathematical concepts and symbols, such as telling the time or distinguishing quantities, money, and pricing.

- **Visual processing:** difficulty interpreting visual information, or understanding visual representations of real-world objects (such as icons).

Learning disabilities

Learning disabilities are common in people of all ages. People with learning disabilities can be sensitive to visual clutter or too many options. They often benefit from supplemental content to aid understanding, such as video and audio to clarify text; or symbols, captions, and transcriptions to make video and audio easier to understand.

Dyslexia is a general term for disorders that result in difficulty in learning to read or interpret words, letters, and other symbols. Dyslexic readers sometimes find it easier to read using specific text and background color combinations. Including a dyslexia-friendly option in your site's preferences will allow people with dyslexia to have a better experience each time they visit your site.

The British Dyslexia Association allows visitors to choose their preferred color palette from a menu at the top of the screen. The menu also relies on symbols over text, making the site easier for people with dyslexia to use. I found the site somewhat hard to use, as I'm not dyslexic and I'm more accustomed to text-based menus. This is a great example of an organization prioritizing the needs of its target audience over other audiences (**FIG 2.3**).

Even though he isn't blind, Sam—like many others with dyslexia—relies on screen readers when using a computer. He finds JAWS's voices too robotic, and prefers NaturalReader by NaturalSoft Ltd. (http://bkaprt.com/afe/02-03/) to hear the text in natural speech form. Sam usually chooses to copy and paste the text he wants read aloud into the software, rather than it reading whole pages. He doesn't want the screen reader to read him the meta information (such as headings and alternative text for images), which distracts him from the primary text.

FIG 2.3: The top of the British Dyslexia Association's site displays an array of accessibility options, including text to speech (http://bkaprt.com/afe/02-02/h).

Literacy

The global adult literacy rate was 85% in 2015, with 757 million illiterate adults—often the result of limited education or learning difficulties. We can also consider that low literacy arises contextually for individuals whose first language is different from the native language of their surroundings.

We can make sites more accessible to people who struggle with literacy by making copy as simple as possible, and including paragraph headings to help people keep their place in the text. When creating forms, offering multiple-choice responses rather than free-form text fields benefits people who have difficulty with writing.

Vestibular disorders and seizures

Vestibular disorders are common, affecting as many as 35% of adults aged forty years or older in the United States. Vestibular disorders are caused by damage to the vestibular system—the parts of the inner ear and brain that control balance and spatial orientation—causing dizziness, vertigo, cognitive confusion, and hearing and visual disturbances.

This often manifests as motion sensitivity on the web. Animations, unconventional scrolling, and parallax backgrounds can cause headaches, dizziness, and nausea, sometimes lasting long after the animation is over.

We can help people with vestibular disorders by giving them control over the animation and motion experiences on our websites. As Val Head wrote in "Designing Safer Web Animation For Motion Sensitivity": "Consider offering an option to turn off, or reduce, motion....Providing what essentially boils down to an alternative way to view that content, or a little extra control, can be a big help for anyone sensitive to motion." (http://bkaprt.com/afe/02-04/). In order to be effective, the option to reduce motion should be presented to users before any animation happens.

Similar considerations can also help prevent seizures. Between 5-10% of people in the developed world will have at least one seizure in their life. About three in 100 people with epilepsy have photosensitive epilepsy, where seizures are triggered by flashing or flickering lights, as well as by high-contrast, striped, or checked patterns.

Obviously, we don't want to trigger seizures in people, and very specific guidelines (http://bkaprt.com/afe/02-05/) exist to help us avoid accidental triggers. Web pages shouldn't contain anything that flashes more than three times in one second. Unless you're creating the world's most annoying banner ad, this is unlikely to be the purposeful result of a design. But animations and hover effects should be checked to ensure that flashing isn't a byproduct when an effect doesn't render as intended.

ENVIRONMENTAL FACTORS

Context has a huge effect on how we use the web, sometimes creating temporary impairments and other obstacles. These include:

- browsing with legacy browsers or operating systems;
- browsing with mobile devices, game consoles, and other non-desktop devices;
- low bandwidth or an intermittent internet connection;
- browsing sites that aren't in our native language, or a familiar culture;
- bright light, rain, or other weather-based conditions;
- noisy or highly distracting environments; and
- ultra-quiet environments (like shared office space, libraries, or a home with sleeping babies).

Such environmental factors suggest that it's not just those with physical impairments who benefit from more accessible websites. The web industry started designing responsive websites so we could be more future-friendly, and if we want to continue to improve people's experiences on the web, accessibility should be at the core of responsive web design.

Browsers

When I started out doing web development, websites could look very different from browser to browser. Development was fraught with hacks to make sites perform similarly across browsers, and we all owed a huge debt to the smart developers who came up with clever ways around bugs. Luckily, with more browsers sharing rendering engines, and better web standards support, websites now render much more consistently across browsers.

Still, many organizations—particularly non-profits and others dependent on public funds—are stuck using old versions of operating systems and browsers because of the software and intranets they need to do their jobs. Proprietary and specialist software can be expensive and time-consuming to upgrade and replace, making it insecure, unstable, and unreliable when used with any future browser releases.

Most modern web developers test their sites in more than one web browser, making cross-browser testing one of the most common forms of accessibility testing: the very act of checking that a site performs well in more than one browser is a way of considering a wider audience.

But a decade ago, smartphones made web browsers on mobile phones usable and useful to a mainstream audience. We quickly optimized our sites for small touch screens. Then many additional devices emerged on the scene.

Devices

Screen size, screen resolution, and screen orientation vary widely from device to device. Input mechanisms may include keyboards, mice, touchscreens, multi-directional pads, motion sensors, or voice control. Some devices have a choice of web browsers, some only have one browser, and often the web is just a "dumb pipe" simply feeding content to the device's own interface. Mobile devices and smartwatches are usually designed to be owned and used by one individual, but game consoles and TVs are often interacted with by multiple people at once. Designing for the web across all these devices is enough to make your head spin.

New sizes and shapes mean we need to design for even more viewport sizes and viewing distances. In other words, we need to continue to design responsively: responsive websites are, by design, accessible to wider audiences.

Context and control

At least 87% of the devices able to access the web are "mobile" now (http://bkaprt.com/afe/02-06/), and that's not including game console browsers (increasingly popular with younger audiences), web-enabled TVs, smartwatches, or virtual reality headsets.

And mobile doesn't mean "on the go," as many of us imagined when mobile devices started becoming popular. Studies have shown that we shouldn't jump to conclusions about user situations based on their devices. A US-based study from AOL and advertising agency BBDO found that 64% of users browse the web on their mobile devices while at home, sitting on their sofas, using their Wi-Fi and broadband (http://bkaprt. com/afe/02-07/). And research from the Interactive Advertising Bureau (IAB) and its Mobile Marketing Center of Excellence (http://bkaprt.com/afe/02-08/) showed that 63% of videos watched on mobile phones were at home and not, in fact, "on the go."

The only reliable statistic we can get back from a person's browser is the width of the viewport. We can't even trust the user agent (the browser telling us its name), as some browsers pretend to be others to get better support from browser-specific styles.

The same is true for assistive technologies, such as screen readers and screen magnifiers. There are no user agent strings for these assistive technologies, leaving us with no idea of how many people are accessing the web with assistive hardware or software. We're left with little choice but to treat these technologies the same way we treat other devices—build for the unknown and test on as many as possible.

The lack of control that we have over devices may seem like a nightmare when creating websites, but it can also be an asset. It encourages us to build more flexible, future-friendly sites that will work on as many devices as possible, making them more likely to support devices with new capabilities. With this wider range of support, our sites are likely to have a much longer lifespan.

Connectivity

The speed of our internet connections has always been a barrier to accessing the web. Prior to the year 2000, in the days of dial-up, the UK had a 56 kb/second speed connection—it would often take sixty seconds to load a web page. In this context, speedy website performance was very important for making a site available at all.

Starting in 2002, broadband connections became more widely available in both the US and UK. Broadband is certainly faster, but not perfect. Connections can be slow due to the distance from the exchange or a poor setup. Have you ever been on the free Wi-Fi at a conference or at an airport? Nothing is guaranteed to slow or crash a Wi-Fi network like a huge number of people trying to connect at the same time.

Similarly, imagine someone working at a coffee shop, using a laptop on a 3G network. When our analytics tell us that the visitor is accessing our site via a desktop browser, we might assume they're on a speedy broadband connection—even though they may be struggling to connect via 3G in an overcrowded city with poor network infrastructure.

And not everybody across the world has access to broadband. Even in the US and UK, high-speed connections are still not widely available in rural and remote areas.

Reliable broadband is common in the tech industry and it's made it easy for us to forget that many of our users may have a slower connection. In striving for better performance, we've become desperate to know the speed of our visitors' connections. To make up for our lack of knowledge, we make assumptions—daft ideas like, "I'll only show the store locations on mobile devices because people who are using mobile phones are *on the go*." But, as we've just seen, this is hardly based in fact. We must give up thinking that we can know people's connective contexts, and enable a web that's accessible regardless of connection speed.

Languages

Like many Brits, I'm terrible at speaking other languages. We privileged native English speakers like to think of English as the lingua franca when we visit other countries, and we tend to act that way on the web as well.

However, the web is worldwide (the clue is in the www!). Not everyone on the web can read and understand English as well as native speakers. We can make our websites much easier to use by making them friendly to other languages.

Localization through translation is the most obvious solution, but it's a tricky business. Professional translation may convey your message to more of your visitors, but it costs a lot of money. A cheaper option is to rely on browser-based autotranslation, such as Google Translate, and website plugins. These can make your website easier to understand, but such translations are imperfect. When Kentucky Fried Chicken (KFC) took their brand to China, they didn't use a native translator, and their famous tagline "Finger lickin' good" became the less appealing "We'll bite your fingers off."

A cost-effective starting point is to simplify your language. Plain language is good usability, making content easier for non-native speakers to understand.

Of course, different audiences dictate different levels of technicality in language. A site aimed at specialist plumbers who know the difference between a stack vent and a wet vent can expect this kind of terminology to be understood. But even technical sites can benefit from the principles of plain language. Writing simply will broaden your audience—and chances are, it'll make automatic translations better, too!

Alphabets and characters

In English, we have an alphabet made up of twenty-six letters, and only use marked letters when borrowing words from other languages, as we do with *naïveté* or *Beyoncé*. Other languages may use accented letters, additional or fewer letters, entirely different alphabets, or even different punctuation marks.

For example, quotation marks vary wildly across Western languages. In English, we primarily use "..." to distinguish a quote, but in many Eastern European languages, the first mark sits on the baseline of the text: „...". In French or Italian, «...» is preferred, but it's »...« in Danish.

A character set (more technically known as *character encoding*) is a defined list of characters that is recognized by software and hardware. For example, the American Standard Code for Information Interchange (ASCII) is a character-encoding standard that maps English letters to numbers that computers understand. For instance, a lowercase *w* is 119 in ASCII. Europe's International Organization for Standardization (ISO) character sets are similar to ASCII, but include additional characters (like *à, ö,* or *æ*) needed for European languages.

If the character sets that make up our alphabets don't contain all the necessary characters for a given language, we can end up with ugly errors in our text. These don't just look bad; they make the words unreadable (FIG 2.4).

Fatta beslut utifrån data.
surveymonkey.com
Ställ rätt frågor om ditt företag och sluta gissa.

FIG 2.4: Most modern browsers will substitute a readable character in place of an error, but the worst-case scenario is ending up with question marks in boxes instead of readable text. This Facebook ad can't deal with the Swedish å, ä or ö.

When selecting a character set for your website, it's always worth double-checking the character sets for foreign-language characters in case the text is translated. (Remember, if a reader is using a translation browser plugin, text can be translated without your input or knowledge.)

When choosing webfonts, you also need to make sure that your fonts contain all the characters required to set the text without errors, regardless of language or alphabet. Most webfont services will allow you to choose the subset of characters embedded in the font. These additional characters can make your fonts larger and slower to load, but have the advantage of making your text much more accessible.

Reading direction

Text in Western languages is read horizontally from left to right. But text in languages such as Arabic, Hebrew, Persian, and Urdu is read horizontally from right to left (FIG 2.5). Reading from

FIG 2.5: BBC News in English (left) uses a left-to-right layout. BBC News in Arabic (right) uses a right-to-left layout.

right to left usually leads to right-aligned text, and a mirror-imaging of the left-to-right page layout.

If you want your site to have international appeal, making it work in different alphabets and for right-to-left readers will go a long way toward improving the usability of your site. You can set the direction of the text using the `dir` attribute in HTML:

```
<body dir="rtl">
```

You can also set the direction of the text using the "direction" property in CSS:

```
body {
    direction: rtl;
}
```

However, it's best to add it to the HTML, as it will still display the text accessible to right-to-left readers if the CSS doesn't load.

Chinese, Japanese, Korean and Mongolian text is mostly read horizontally from left to right on the web, but more traditional or expressive text is often set vertically to be read from top to bottom and right to left. To set the vertical text direction we can use `writing-mode: vertical-rl;` in our CSS.

Reading a page in an unfamiliar layout can be very slow and challenging, but we can change the text direction depending upon the language displayed. See Chapter 5 for HTML and CSS examples.

FIG 2.6: Domestic Violence UK has a sticky "Hide Site" button at the top of every page which quickly redirects the page to Google, in case victims of abuse are being watched or monitored by abusive partners.

Space and context

As designers and developers, it can be easy to get caught up in the interaction inside screens and forget how much the environment outside of screens and devices affects the experience. With access to the internet becoming increasingly mobile, somebody could be trying to use your site up the side of a mountain in the driving snow, or on a desert trail in the burning hot sun. High contrasts between text and background colors will make a great difference to text readability in severe weather conditions!

But environments aren't just about the weather and light, they can also be about who's in the room with you. If you're working in a public space and don't have headphones, you may not want to play audio content or videos with sound. If you're trying to get work done in a noisy or disruptive space, you may not be able to hear audio or video, even with headphones. The considerations for these contexts are similar to those for hearing loss—you'd probably prefer subtitles, captions, or another text alternative for the content.

Using the web can also be a personal experience requiring privacy. Sites can be made more usable in these situations (and benefit everybody) by making their information clear and easy to locate, and even tailoring the experience to specific stress cases (**FIG 2.6**). Sara Wachter-Boettcher and Eric Meyer explain how to identify these stress cases and incorporate compassion into your design process in their book, *Design for Real Life* (http://bkaprt.com/afe/02-09/).

Sharing devices can also reveal potential problems. Someone who's been looking for information on a medical condition doesn't want personalized ads for therapies and medications following their partner or family member around the web. Respect the privacy of your visitors by default, and ensure you aren't leaking their information to third parties who may not be so respectful.

MEETING NEEDS

Statistics are handy when you're trying to show your boss how many people can't access your site if you don't make it accessible. But statistics can't tell the whole story, or show the extent of the value that accessibility can offer.

Statistics often only apply to people who are registered with long-term or permanent disabilities, as the data is largely gathered for insurance or welfare systems. More detailed data is hard to gather because impairments are unpredictable, and often impermanent. We might have an accident or illness that affects us temporarily. We might struggle earlier or later in the day. And as we age, we're more likely to experience different levels of visual, auditory, motor, and cognitive impairments (and the aging population is increasing).

There are so many little physiological factors that affect the way people interact with the web that we can't afford to make any assumptions based on our own limited experiences. In the next chapter, we'll look at how setting goals for your product's accessibility can help you avoid assumptions and start meeting real needs.

3

PLANNING FOR ACCESSIBILITY

INCORPORATING ACCESSIBILITY FROM the beginning is almost always easier, more effective, and less expensive than making accessibility improvements as a separate project. In fact, building accessibility into your project and processes has a wealth of business benefits. If you're looking to make the case for accessibility—to yourself, to coworkers, or to bosses and clients—you might start here:

- **Findability and ease of use:** In the broadest terms, accessibility can make it easier for anyone to find, access, and use a website successfully. By ensuring better usability for all, accessibility boosts a site's effectiveness and increases its potential audience.
- **Competitive edge:** The wider your audience, the greater your reach and commercial appeal. When a site is more accessible than other sites in the same market, it can lead to preferential treatment from people who struggled to use competitors' sites. If a site is translated, or has more simply written content that improves automated translation,

increased accessibility can lead to a larger audience by reaching people who speak other languages.

- **Lower costs:** Accessible websites can cut costs in other areas of a business. On a more accessible site, more customers can complete more tasks and transactions online, rather than needing to talk to a representative one-to-one.
- **Legal protection:** In a few countries, an accessible site is required by law for organizations in certain sectors—and organizations with inaccessible sites can be sued for discrimination against people with disabilities.

Once you've made the case for incorporating accessibility into your work, the next step is to integrate an accessibility mindset into your processes. Include accessibility by default by giving accessibility proper consideration at every step in a product's lifecycle.

BUILDING YOUR TEAM

Web accessibility is the responsibility of everyone who has a hand in the design of a site. Design includes all of the decisions we make when we create a product—not just the pretty bits, but the decisions about how it works and who it's for. This means everybody involved in the project is a designer of some sort.

Each specialist is responsible for a basic understanding of their work's impact on accessibility, and on their colleagues' work. For example, independent consultant Anne Gibson says that information architects should keep an eye on the markup:

> We may or may not be responsible for writing the HTML, but if the developers we're working with don't produce semantic structure, then they're not actually representing the structures that we're building in our designs.

Leadership and support

While we should all be attentive to how accessibility impacts our specialism, it's important to have leadership to help determine priorities and key areas where the product's overall accessibility needs improvement. Project manager Henny Swan (user experience and design lead at the Paciello Group, and previously of the BBC) recommends that accessibility be owned by product managers. The product managers must consider how web accessibility affects what the organization does, understand the organization's legal duties, and consider the potential business benefits.

Sometimes people find themselves stuck within a company or team that doesn't value accessibility. But armed with knowledge and expertise about accessibility, we can still do good work as individuals, and have a positive effect on the accessibility of a site. For example, a designer can ensure all the background and foreground text colors on their site are in good contrast, making text easier to distinguish and read.

Unfortunately, without the support and understanding of our colleagues, the accessibility of a site can easily be let down in other areas. While the colors could be accessible, if another designer has decided that the body text should be set at 12 pixels, the content will still be hard to read.

When accessibility is instituted as a company-wide practice, rather than merely observed by a few people within a team, it will inevitably be more successful. When everybody understands the importance of accessibility and their role in the project, we can make great websites.

Professional development

When you're just starting to learn about accessibility, people in your organization will need to learn new skills and undertake training to do accessibility well.

Outside experts can often provide thorough training, with course material tailor-made to your organization. Teams can also develop their accessibility skills by learning the basics through web- and book-based research, and by attending relevant conferences and other events.

Both formal training and independent practice will cost time away from other work, but in return you'll get rapid improvements in a team's accessibility skills. New skills might mean initially slower site development and testing while people are still getting their heads around unfamiliar tools, techniques, and ways of thinking. Don't be disheartened! It doesn't take long for the regular practice of new skills to become second nature.

You might also need to hire in outside expertise to assist you in particular areas of accessibility—it's worth considering the capabilities of your team during budgeting and decide whether additional training and help are needed. Especially when just starting out, many organizations hire consultants or new employees with accessibility expertise to help with research and testing.

When you're trying to find the right expert for your organization's needs, avoid just bashing "accessibility expert" into a search engine and hoping for good luck. Accessibility blogs and informational websites (see the Resources section) are probably the best place to start, as you can often find individuals and organizations who are great at teaching and communicating accessibility. The people who run accessibility websites often provide consultancy services, or will have recommendations for the best people they know.

SCOPING THE PROJECT

At the beginning of a project, you'll need to make many decisions that will have an impact on accessibility efforts and approaches, including:

- What is the purpose of your product?
- Who are the target audiences for your product? What are their needs, restrictions, and technology preferences?
- What are the goals and tasks that your product enables the user to complete?
- What is the experience your product should provide for each combination of user group and user goal?
- How can accessibility be integrated during production?
- Which target platforms, browsers, operating systems and assistive technologies should you test the product on?

If you have answers to these questions—possibly recorded more formally in an accessibility policy (which we'll look at later in this chapter)—you'll have something to refer to when making design decisions throughout the creation and maintenance of the product.

Keep in mind that rigid initial specifications and proposals can cause problems when a project involves research and iterative design. Being flexible during the creation of a product will allow you to make decisions based on new information, respond to any issues that arise during testing, and ensure that the launched product genuinely meets people's needs.

If you're hiring someone outside your organization to produce your site, you need to convey the importance of accessibility to the project. Whether you're a project manager writing requirements, a creative agency writing a brief, or a freelance consultant scoping your intent, making accessibility a requirement will ensure there's no ambiguity. Documenting your success criteria and sharing it with other people can help everyone understand your aims, both inside and outside your organization.

Budgeting

Accessibility isn't a line item in an estimate or a budget—it's an underlying practice that affects every aspect of a project.

Building an accessible site doesn't necessarily cost more money or time than an inaccessible site, but some of the costs are different: it costs money to train your team or build alternative materials like transcripts or translations. It's wise to consider all potential costs from the beginning and factor them into the product budget so they're not a surprise or considered an "extra cost" when they could benefit a wide audience. You wouldn't add a line item to make a site performant, so don't do it for accessibility either.

If you've got a very small budget, rather than picking and choosing particular elements that leave some users out in favor of others, consider the least expensive options that enable the widest possible audience to access your site. For example, making a carousel that can be manipulated using only the keyboard will only benefit people using keyboard navigation. On the other hand, designing a simpler interface without a carousel will benefit everyone using the site.

Ultimately, the cost of accessibility depends on the size of the project, team, and whether you're retrofitting an existing product or creating a new product. The more projects you work on, the better you'll be able to estimate the impact and costs of accessibility.

RESEARCH

Research can help us gain a better understanding of the people who will be using the site. It gives us a much stronger foundation on which to make informed decisions—about accessibility, but also about every other aspect of a site's design. As Erika Hall explains in *Just Enough Research* (http://bkaprt.com/afe/03-01/):

> Discovering how and why people behave as they do and what opportunities that presents for your business or organization will open the way to more innovative and appropriate design solutions than asking how they feel or merely tweaking your current design based on analytics.

Research isn't just asking people what they like. If you ask people for their favorite color, and Suzy likes white but Aneel likes blue, that's not going to help you design your website. Instead, research helps uncover people's motivations and habits and how those might translate to their use of our sites.

Researching accessibility forces you to delve into the full range of your audiences' needs—including differing impairments and environments—which will significantly enrich your plan for an accessible product.

Researching with real users

Online testing can be a good option for small teams with tight budgets. Additionally, in *A Web for Everyone*, Sarah Horton and Whitney Quesenbery observe that "including people with disabilities in user experience design is even easier if you're doing your research or testing online." This makes a lot of sense: it's easier to find a wider range of people if your search can be global.

If you have the time and budget, face-to-face research has a lot more benefits. Seeing real people use your product lets you understand their environment, context, needs, and behaviors. You can see exactly how they interact with their hardware and software, and you won't need to rely on people accurately reporting their own behavior.

For example, Emily may type a message on her mobile device using one hand, tapping letters out with her thumb. Annie types a message by holding the device in her left hand and tapping the letters out with her right index finger. Jessica dictates all her messages using voice recognition. All three of them probably think the way they use their mobile device is "normal" and not worth mentioning. But interaction designers will notice that the way they're holding the device effects the area of the screen they can comfortably reach. People in different roles in our organizations will be better equipped to notice details relevant to their own work.

This is why it's also valuable to have a wide range of roles involved in research. Just as with accessibility, research isn't the sole responsibility of one person or one role. Everyone should be involved in research from beginning to end.

Recruiting people with disabilities

Recruiting people for research is hard work. Recruiting people with disabilities is even harder.

We're often told to maximize the efficiency of our research by talking to people who fit our target audience. This is good practice, but we must ensure we avoid the "we don't have any users with disabilities" pitfall. That's a dark path that risks ending in disability discrimination lawsuits.

To make it simple: when you're researching your target audience, always include people with disabilities and impairments. They're likely to have the same motivations and habits as people without disabilities, but their needs will bring potential usability and accessibility issues to the fore much more quickly.

It can be difficult to research a broad enough group of people, and you won't be able to learn about every impairment or combinations of impairments. Some impairments may not affect how someone uses your site. However, you can only understand how to make your site accessible to your target audience if you record the requirements of people with specialist needs.

In *Just Ask: Integrating Accessibility Throughout Design*, Shawn Henry reminds us to look at people with disabilities as individuals, rather than grouping them together (http://bkaprt.com/afe/03-02/):

> Be careful not to assume that feedback from one person with a disability applies to all people with disabilities. A person with a disability doesn't necessarily know how other people with the same disability interact with products, nor know enough about other disabilities to provide valid guidance on other accessibility issues. Just as you would not make design decisions based on feedback from just one user, don't make accessibility decisions based only on the recommendations of one person with a disability. What works for one person might not work for everyone with that disability or for people with other disabilities.

An important part of research with people using assistive technologies is to separate user requirements (user analysis) from technology needs (workflow analysis.) Léonie Watson, communications director and principal engineer at The Paciello Group, says that designers often conflate a particular assistive technology with a particular disability—for example, assuming that everyone using a screen reader is blind. The technology is a key part of the research, but it isn't the same as the requirements of the individual.

Interacting with participants

In *Just Ask*, Henry has great advice on how to provide for, and interact with, people with disabilities in your research and testing: treat people with disabilities in the same way you'd treat anybody else.

Don't make assumptions about what people want or need. Stick to information relevant to the participant's interaction with your site. And for crying out loud, get to know them before you ask any personal questions. You might be curious, but it really is rude to ask, "Have you always been like that?" Once you've welcomed your participant and introduced the research you're doing, "How long have you been using a screen reader?" might be a relevant question to ask. And it may get you some further contextual information if the participant is comfortable talking to you.

Learning from your research

The work doesn't stop once you've done all this research. Next you have to work out how to make it useful. You need to gather all your data together and look for meaningful patterns in your observations. The goals, priorities, and motivations of people with impairments are likely to be similar to anybody else, but their barriers and tools may vary. Those barriers and tools will in turn affect the actions they take to meet their goal.

Watson emphasizes that it's important to gather quantitative data during research and requirements gathering, so you truly understand how many people may benefit from the improvements:

> It's often the case within the disabled community that there are a few vocal people, with very decided opinions about how something should be done for their particular group. Sometimes those opinions are robust, other times they're not—and all too often they're to the exclusion of people with other kinds of disability.

Research is cumulative. From project to project, you'll learn more, and be more generally informed. That doesn't mean you'll need to do less research on each new project—every project comes with its own unique context. But it does mean that every time you start the research on a new project, you'll be aware of more effective research methods and what's worked for you before.

PRODUCTION AND DEVELOPMENT

Whether you're building a system from scratch, or using existing frameworks and libraries, the technologies you use will have a huge impact on the accessibility of a product.

Being wary of the potential accessibility benefits and pitfalls of each component will help you assess its suitability for your project—and should be the responsibility of the developer to research and understand. Using frameworks or components that have a focus on accessibility, and are grounded in research and testing, can save you time and resources in the long run.

As an easy example, you may decide that Adobe Flash is not a suitable component for your system because fewer browsers come with the required plugin, particularly on mobile devices. Flash also has difficulty communicating with the accessibility layer on operating systems that provides access to assistive technologies.

And since accessibility begins with accessible content, the content management system (CMS) you choose is incredibly important. A good CMS should enable the content creator to produce content in a way that's accessible to both the creator and the consumer.

Testing on devices

It's worth noting that obtaining assistive technologies will make up some of your setup costs. Buying and testing with these assistive technologies throughout the development process will help developers, designers, and others understand how people interact with their work.

Many assistive technologies are inexpensive or free and make for easy initial testing. You may need to budget funds to buy other devices that don't fall into the assistive technology category, if you don't already use a device lab or test across multiple platforms. We'll discuss testing more in Chapter 6.

MAINTENANCE

We all know about those dangerous little, last-minute fixes when you're pushing a site live. Maybe your marketing team has come up with a great concept for a landing page a week before launch: it's rich with images and video and parallax scrolling! It tells a beautiful story of your organization, and the designer has created a working prototype that's just stunning. You're all so caught up in the whirlwind of the bewitching design that you forget to make the HTML accessible, but no one on the team uses assistive technology so nobody notices, and you launch it anyway.

You need to watch out for these gotchas, because you may not realize that you've done something to compromise accessibility until later down the line. Always test after launching or updating to ensure that last-minute launch details don't undermine accessibility.

Again, having an accessibility policy will help you maintain high standards and prevent you from compromising on the basics, so let's explore exactly what an accessibility policy is and how to make one.

Accessibility policies

Good accessibility policies are informed by extensive research into the needs of your target audience, and will help:

- ensure everyone in your organization understands the importance of accessibility,
- standardize the way your organization approaches accessibility, and
- prioritize user groups when handling competing needs.

The term "policy" is slightly misleading corporate-speak: an accessibility policy can be anything from a formal document that shows compliance, to a set of standards, to a casual statement that outlines your organization's approach and intentions toward the accessibility of your site.

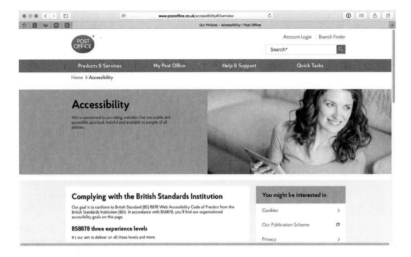

FIG 3.1: The Post Office's accessibility policy puts "Complying with the British Standards Institution" up top, but further down there's more focus on the people using their site.

Guidelines in your accessibility policy should be:

- clear and simply written, so anyone in your organization can refer to your policy and understand the implications and their role;
- hierarchical, so needs are prioritized as primary, secondary, etc.; and
- testable, so you can easily determine whether your site is sufficiently accessible.

The testable criteria in your accessibility policy could be based on the Web Content Accessibility Guidelines (WCAG) 2.0 criteria, or criteria from the standards local to your country.

You can see a great example of an accessibility policy on the UK's Post Office website (http://bkaprt.com/afe/03-03/). The Post Office's accessibility policy moves from general to more specific aims (**FIG 3.1**), covering:

- goals for the website experience,
- goals for site's accessibility,

- the individual responsible for the policy and its implementation, and
- the accessibility of their non-digital products and services.

Accessibility policies, much like style guides, don't always have to be made public—their primary value is as internal documents. That said, posting them publicly shows your commitment to accessibility and lets visitors know what they can expect from your site or agency.

JUSTIFYING YOUR ACCESSIBILITY DECISIONS

At each stage of your process, you'll have to make decisions about accessibility. Building your team's accessibility skills, grounding your work in user research, and maintaining an accessibility policy that outlines your approach will not only help you make strategic decisions, but justify them as well—to yourself, your clients, and your stakeholders.

Now let's look at how we can make our sites more accessible today—starting with content and design.

4

CONTENT AND DESIGN

DESIGN DECISIONS MADE in the name of accessibility generally benefit everyone, because *all technology is assistive*. This is in fact the title of a wonderful essay by artist and design researcher Sara Hendren (http://bkaprt.com/afe/04-01/), who reminds us that "all people, over the course of their lives, traffic between times of relative independence and dependence."

Hendren asks, "What technology are you using that's *not assistive?*" Our keyboards and mice assist us in communicating with a computer. Our headphones enable us to hear audio in our own spaces without disrupting those around us. Our phones give us the knowledge of the entire web in our pockets. Technology enables us all, and can give us a better experience of the world around us.

To improve the experience for everyone, we can focus on the usability of the web across four broad parameters:

1. **Visual**: make it easy to see.
2. **Auditory**: make it easy to hear.
3. **Motor**: make it easy to interact with.
4. **Cognitive**: make it easy to understand.

While these examples illustrate just a few benefits, they show that accessibility goals are also usability goals. Good accessibility is good usability.

AFFORDANCES AND CONVENTIONS

Affordances are how objects suggest the interactions that can be performed with them—ideally in a way that's recognizable by users. For example, when we turn on a new computer for the first time, we look for a button with the power icon. We expect a button because we're accustomed to the on-off function of hardware operated by a physical input. We look for the power icon because it's a conventional symbol used in electronics (**FIG 4.1**). Over time, these affordances become conventions we can rely on, both as designers and as users.

Usability can be compromised when designers abandon conventions because we've decided to "redefine" how something is usually done. Very occasionally, this can result in a new innovation that genuinely redefines and reshapes behavior, but it usually just makes a really unique mess (**FIG 4.2**).

On the web, using conventions well makes for a gentler learning curve for new visitors. A common convention is to design interactions using visual metaphors, to make the design imitate a similar real-world artifact. The most prevalent and successful use of a visual metaphor on the web is the button. Buttons trigger a behavior, such as submitting a form or changing a setting, because buttons in the physical space trigger behaviors, too, such as turning lights on and off. Browsers commonly use a simple three-dimensional appearance to give a button on the web an affordance that suggests, "Press me and I'll respond" (**FIG 4.3**).

Alas, a visual metaphor can backfire if it looks like one object but performs like another. One of my pet peeves is when a link to another site is made to look like a button. The button style is usually chosen over a conventional link style to draw more attention to the link, but the conventional behavior of a button is to perform an action within the site, not to redirect the user

FIG 4.1: A button with the power icon is the first thing we look for when we turn on our electronics. Photograph courtesy of Anssi Koskinen (http://bkaprt.com/afe/04-02/).

FIG 4.2: Sideways scrolling websites had their peak in the late 00s. It certainly makes for an attention-grabbing surprise, but horizontal scrolling can be difficult if you use a mouse for scrolling—very few mice have horizontal scroll wheels.

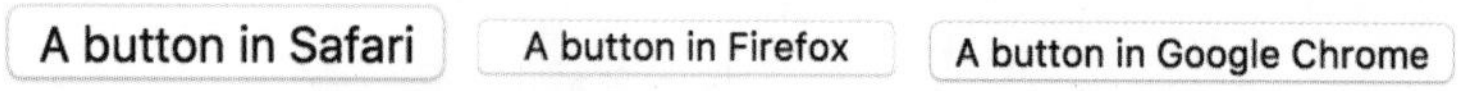

A button in Safari   A button in Firefox   A button in Google Chrome

FIG 4.3: An HTML `<button>` in Safari, Firefox, and Google Chrome is rendered slightly differently depending on the browser's default style, but they all look buttonesque.

FIG 4.4: Coupon code sites often style links to other sites as calls to action. This "Click to Redeem" is just an affiliate link to the Happy Feet homepage.

to a different location. It's like turning on your bedroom light only to find you've been teleported to your kitchen (**FIG 4.4**).

Affordances and conventions should inform the design and content of your sites. Content could be text, images, video, audio, or interactive experiences. Ensuring that it's all designed to be usable and accessible is paramount—starting with how the user finds their way around the content.

NAVIGATION AND WAYFINDING

Without a strong information architecture, people can easily get lost. We need to provide consistent ways to help people find content and determine where they are, regardless of what page they're visiting and their position on that page.

Navigation bar

Most sites use a navigation bar at the top of the page that contains a list of links to a site's main areas. You'll find many forms of navigation on the web, but this is probably the most common. However, the navigation bar doesn't just provide a means

FIG 4.5: The United Nations homepage uses subnavigation which doubles as a description of what you can find in each section.

to travel around your site—it can also provide a summary of what a visitor can expect to find (**FIG 4.5**).

Subnavigation bars, sidebars, and footers also provide visitors with a better idea of what's available on your site. However, it's difficult to rely on these navigation patterns as they're not consistent from one site to another and people may not always understand where to look.

When the navigation reflects the information architecture of your site, it gives people a better understanding of where they need to go and offers a preview of other information they might find relevant or interesting. Navigation bars work best when they offer a brief snapshot; they become unwieldy if the list of links they contain is too long.

Once we've established what you want to include in your navigation elements, we can consider the text for each link. With usability in mind, and to paraphrase Steve Krug's *Don't Make Me Think!*, we've learned it's best to make navigation descriptive and concise. It's hard for a new visitor to understand what to expect from a site archiving interviews about

FIG 4.6: Without further explanation, a visitor can only really be assured of the contents in the "Clips" section.

FIG 4.7: Replacing "Playlists" with "Themes," and "Minds" with "People" makes more sense within the context of a games industry interview archive.

the games industry when the navigation lists "Clips, Minds, Playlists, Conversations" (FIG 4.6). When we use terminology that's easy to understand, more visitors will be able to find what they want (FIG 4.7).

Mystery meat

Every now and again, I come across an "alternative" navigation where a designer has decided they can subvert existing conventions and provide someone with a whole new experience (FIG 4.8). Unfortunately, these experiences often don't succeed because deciphering the navigation proves too bothersome. People would rather spend their time elsewhere.

Back in the heyday of Adobe Flash, there was a lot of experimentation around navigation using hovering, dragging, and some kind of logic puzzle you had to solve to navigate the site. While I'm not averse to experimentation and innovation—we all want to make better web experiences—you'd need to have an extraordinarily good reason as to why existing conventions don't work for your site if you insist on going that route (FIG 4.9).

FIG 4.8: Hovering over different parts of the green map on this theme park's site brings up different navigation links, including the terrifying-looking "Nautic Jet." The buttons down the side do provide an alternative navigation. But why have two of the same navigation? (http://www.freizeitparkherne.de/overview/overview.html)

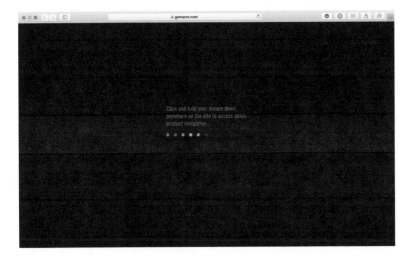

FIG 4.9: Why not always have "quick product navigation" on the site? Why is there a loading bar? I have so many questions!

If your navigation needs an explanation, you should probably rethink it—and consider returning to well-established conventions.

Titles and breadcrumbs

Another role of navigation is orientation—helping someone determine where they are. Search results often bring people to an internal page on a site that's not listed in the main navigation elements. A visitor's first stop when identifying where they are on a site is usually the page title. A highlighted or "active" style in the navigation can also help people understand where they are. (**FIG 4.10**).

On large sites, breadcrumbs are often used to help visitors understand the relationship between the page they're viewing and other areas of the site (**FIG 4.11**). Breadcrumbs can be particularly valuable to people who have difficulty remembering where they've been or what they're trying to accomplish.

When I worked with the Alzheimer's Society on a responsive redesign of their site, we paid particular attention to the navigation. Research and usability testing on their site indicated that breadcrumbs were especially valuable to visitors who had symptoms of dementia, including memory loss and confusion. But, again, all audiences benefit from clear wayfinding signals that orient them within a site.

Links

Links are as old as the web, so long-standing conventions and standards have developed around them. Most browsers render links in blue text with an underline by default. If the link has been visited before, the text appears purple (**FIG 4.12**).

These common styles make links easy to recognize on a page. Over the years, fewer sites have stuck to the blue color standard, but most still use the underline to distinguish a link from non-interactive text. The contrast between link text and regular text is the key consideration. Finding links in a body of text shouldn't be a cruel game where the reader has to hover over every word to find them.

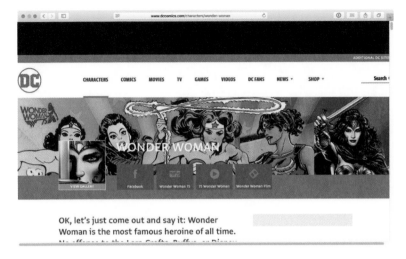

FIG 4.10: The DC Comics site navigation uses a blue bar under the active navigation link to remind you which section you're currently viewing.

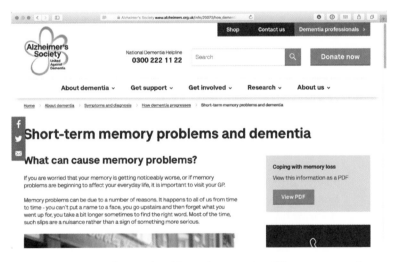

FIG 4.11: Not everyone who uses the Alzheimer's Society site will have symptoms of dementia—a visitor could be learning about a loved one's illness. But clear and useful navigation is valuable in times of stress.

Link   Link   Visited link   Active link

FIG 4.12: The humble link in all its default style glory.

FIG 4.13: Google search results looks more crowded with links underlined (left) than when the links are just big and blue (right).

Two years ago, Google decided to drop the underlined style in their links (http://bkaprt.com/afe/04-03/). The lack of underlines makes the page layout appear much cleaner and the text slightly easier to read (FIG 4.13).

Making a change this significant was a big deal for Google: they could lose a lot of page clicks—one of their sources of income—if people couldn't distinguish the links from the rest of the text. However, Google's other design decisions ensured they stuck with enough conventions to keep the links obvious:

- bright blue link color, consistent with many other sites
- underline visible on hover
- visible URL on every search result item

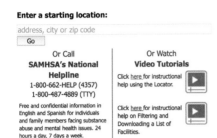

Enter a starting location:

address, city or zip code

Go

Or Call
SAMHSA's National Helpline
1-800-662-HELP (4357)
1-800-487-4889 (TTY)

Free and confidential information in English and Spanish for individuals and family members facing substance abuse and mental health issues. 24 hours a day, 7 days a week.

Or Watch
Video Tutorials

Click here for instructional help using the Locator.

Click here for instructional help on Filtering and Downloading a List of Facilities.

FIG 4.14: Both links for these video tutorials are just labelled "here." (And not everyone even clicks! As we saw in Chapter 1, many people use different input devices.)

Link language

I mentioned earlier that screen readers can jump between links on a page. Navigating through a page full of links using a screen reader can be tiresome—or worse, useless. "Click here, click here, click here" is often all you'll hear.

The "click here" repetition is a common issue caused by nondescript link text (**FIG 4.14**). This often crops up in sentences ending with a call to action, such as "To get in contact with our team, click here."

The problem is that using "click here" as the language for your links renders the links meaningless for those with screen readers as well as those without. Descriptive linking, instead, helps links make sense out of context, and provides users with a sense of where the link will take them or what will happen after they click. "Read the full article" is a lot more descriptive than "Click here."

Descriptive linking also helps simplify your writing. "To get in contact with our team, click here" can be simplified to "Get in contact with our team." Or: "Last week we posted a review of Murder in The Clouds. You can read that review here" can be simplified to "Last week we posted a review of Murder in The Clouds."

Writing this way takes practice, but your readers (and listeners) will thank you for it.

WRITING

Writing great copy comprises more than good spelling, grammar, and text in a coherent order. The best sites have content that is understandable, useful, and appropriate for its audience.

Hierarchy and structure

Accessible content begins with well-structured copy. At the page level, structure helps readers understand which text on a page is most important. Using clear and concise headings makes it easy for someone to skim the page and understand the information they're likely to find (**FIG 4.15**).

If your text contains lists, separate them out from paragraph text to make them clear. The different structure will also break up the page, providing space for the reader to rest (**FIG 4.16**).

A well-structured and easily navigable page also looks less intimidating. For someone who struggles to read and understand text, a clear content hierarchy could be the difference between wanting to read a page or closing the browser tab because the page doesn't look worth the effort.

Long lines of text can be hard to read, as readers may struggle to read continuously without a break, sometimes finding it hard to remember what they read at the beginning of the sentence. Punctuation can help break sentences into smaller chunks, but short sentences are much easier to read.

Everyone can benefit from short, easy-to-read sentences and well-structured page content. Take my brother Sam, for example. Reading requires a lot of concentration for him, so Sam tends to read in short bursts, returning to the same page multiple times. Content that is split into a clear hierarchy, with obvious headings, helps him easily return to his previous place.

His ideal text format is the small bits of trivia presented on the IMDb (Internet Movie Database) website, because they're relatively easy for him to memorize. The IMDb movie pages are well-structured, with clearly bordered sections and large bold titles. Visual cues like hyperlinks help Sam quickly find related content. Similarities in layout from one page to another

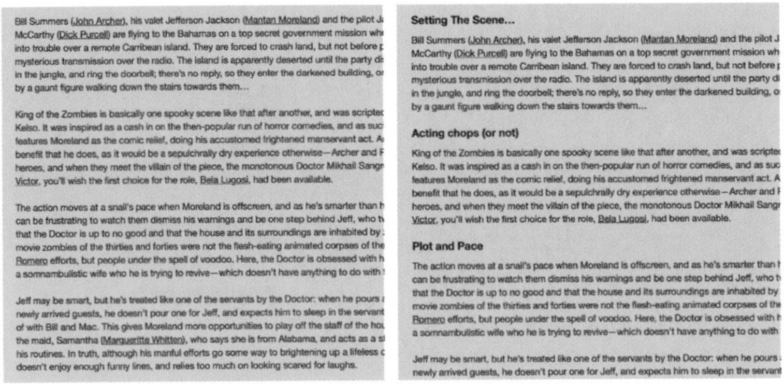

Bill Summers (John Archer), his valet Jefferson Jackson (Mantan Moreland) and the pilot J
McCarthy (Dick Purcell) are flying to the Bahamas on a top secret government mission wh
into trouble over a remote Carribean island. They are forced to crash land, but not before
mysterious transmission over the radio. The island is apparently deserted until the party d
in the jungle, and ring the doorbell; there's no reply, so they enter the darkened building, o
by a gaunt figure walking down the stairs towards them...

King of the Zombies is basically one spooky scene like that after another, and was scripte
Kelso. It was inspired as a cash in on the then-popular run of horror comedies, and as suc
features Moreland as the comic relief, doing his accustomed frightened manservant act. A
benefit that he does, as it would be a sepulchrally dry experience otherwise—Archer and F
heroes, and when they meet the villain of the piece, the monotonous Doctor Mikhail Sangr
Victor, you'll wish the first choice for the role, Bela Lugosi, had been available.

The action moves at a snail's pace when Moreland is offscreen, and as he's smarter than h
can be frustrating to watch them dismiss his warnings and be one step behind Jeff, who t
that the Doctor is up to no good and that the house and its surroundings are inhabited by
movie zombies of the thirties and forties were not the flesh-eating animated corpses of the
Romero efforts, but people under the spell of voodoo. Here, the Doctor is obsessed with h
a somnambulistic wife who he is trying to revive—which doesn't have anything to do with

Jeff may be smart, but he's treated like one of the servants by the Doctor: when he pours
newly arrived guests, he doesn't pour one for Jeff, and expects him to sleep in the servant
of with Bill and Mac. This gives Moreland more opportunities to play off the staff of the hou
the maid, Samantha (Marguerite Whitten), who says she is from Alabama, and acts as a s
his routines. In truth, although his manful efforts go some way to brightening up a lifeless
doesn't enjoy enough funny lines, and relies too much on looking scared for laughs.

Setting The Scene...

Bill Summers (John Archer), his valet Jefferson Jackson (Mantan Moreland) and the pilot J
McCarthy (Dick Purcell) are flying to the Bahamas on a top secret government mission wh
into trouble over a remote Carribean island. They are forced to crash land, but not before
mysterious transmission over the radio. The island is apparently deserted until the party d
in the jungle, and ring the doorbell; there's no reply, so they enter the darkened building, o
by a gaunt figure walking down the stairs towards them...

Acting chops (or not)

King of the Zombies is basically one spooky scene like that after another, and was scripte
Kelso. It was inspired as a cash in on the then-popular run of horror comedies, and as suc
features Moreland as the comic relief, doing his accustomed frightened manservant act. A
benefit that he does, as it would be a sepulchrally dry experience otherwise—Archer and F
heroes, and when they meet the villain of the piece, the monotonous Doctor Mikhail Sangr
Victor, you'll wish the first choice for the role, Bela Lugosi, had been available.

Plot and Pace

The action moves at a snail's pace when Moreland is offscreen, and as he's smarter than h
can be frustrating to watch them dismiss his warnings and be one step behind Jeff, who t
that the Doctor is up to no good and that the house and its surroundings are inhabited by
movie zombies of the thirties and forties were not the flesh-eating animated corpses of the
Romero efforts, but people under the spell of voodoo. Here, the Doctor is obsessed with h
a somnambulistic wife who he is trying to revive—which doesn't have anything to do with

Jeff may be smart, but he's treated like one of the servants by the Doctor: when he pours
newly arrived guests, he doesn't pour one for Jeff, and expects him to sleep in the servant

FIG 4.15: Body text with no headings (left), and with headings breaking up the text (right). I know which one I'd rather read!

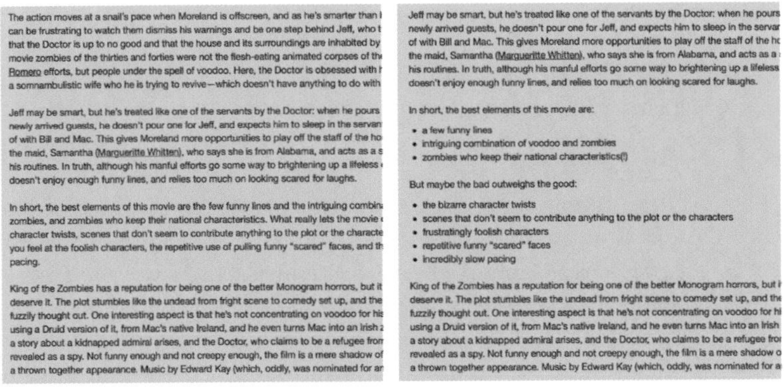

The action moves at a snail's pace when Moreland is offscreen, and as he's smarter than h
can be frustrating to watch them dismiss his warnings and be one step behind Jeff, who t
that the Doctor is up to no good and that the house and its surroundings are inhabited by
movie zombies of the thirties and forties were not the flesh-eating animated corpses of the
Romero efforts, but people under the spell of voodoo. Here, the Doctor is obsessed with h
a somnambulistic wife who he is trying to revive—which doesn't have anything to do with

Jeff may be smart, but he's treated like one of the servants by the Doctor: when he pours
newly arrived guests, he doesn't pour one for Jeff, and expects him to sleep in the servan
of with Bill and Mac. This gives Moreland more opportunities to play off the staff of the ho
the maid, Samantha (Marguerite Whitten), who says she is from Alabama, and acts as a s
his routines. In truth, although his manful efforts go some way to brightening up a lifeless
doesn't enjoy enough funny lines, and relies too much on looking scared for laughs.

In short, the best elements of this movie are the few funny lines and the intriguing combin
zombies, and zombies who keep their national characteristics. What really lets the movie
character twists, scenes that don't seem to contribute anything to the plot or the characte
you feel at the foolish characters, the repetitive use of pulling funny "scared" faces, and th
pacing.

King of the Zombies has a reputation for being one of the better Monogram horrors, but it
deserve it. The plot stumbles like the undead from fright scene to comedy set up, and the
fuzzily thought out. One interesting aspect is that he's not concentrating on voodoo for his
using a Druid version of it, from Mac's native Ireland, and he even turns Mac into an Irish
a story about a kidnapped admiral arises, and the Doctor, who claims to be a refugee fron
revealed as a spy. Not funny enough and not creepy enough, the film is a mere shadow of
a thrown together appearance. Music by Edward Kay (which, oddly, was nominated for ar

Jeff may be smart, but he's treated like one of the servants by the Doctor: when he pours
newly arrived guests, he doesn't pour one for Jeff, and expects him to sleep in the servar
of with Bill and Mac. This gives Moreland more opportunities to play off the staff of the hc
the maid, Samantha (Marguerite Whitten), who says she is from Alabama, and acts as a
his routines. In truth, although his manful efforts go some way to brightening up a lifeless
doesn't enjoy enough funny lines, and relies too much on looking scared for laughs.

In short, the best elements of this movie are:

- a few funny lines
- intriguing combination of voodoo and zombies
- zombies who keep their national characteristics(!)

But maybe the bad outweighs the good:

- the bizarre character twists
- scenes that don't seem to contribute anything to the plot or the characters
- frustratingly foolish characters
- repetitive funny "scared" faces
- incredibly slow pacing

King of the Zombies has a reputation for being one of the better Monogram horrors, but i
deserve it. The plot stumbles like the undead from fright scene to comedy set up, and the
fuzzily thought out. One interesting aspect is that he's not concentrating on voodoo for hi
using a Druid version of it, from Mac's native Ireland, and he even turns Mac into an Irish
a story about a kidnapped admiral arises, and the Doctor, who claims to be a refugee fro
revealed as a spy. Not funny enough and not creepy enough, the film is a mere shadow o
a thrown together appearance. Music by Edward Kay (which, oddly, was nominated for a

FIG 4.16: Bulleted lists and numbered lists don't just make the items easier to read, they also break up long blocks of text, making the reading experience less intimidating.

help him remember the area of the page where he'll find the information he wants without having to read everything else on the page first—for instance, he knows he will always find the "Storyline" below the "Cast List" on an IMDb movie page (**FIG 4.17**).

FIG 4.17: Every IMDb movie page is structured with content in the same order, and with the same headings.

Plain language

Clear, simple, and concise language makes the most accessible text. Concise writing comes with practice, and makes text much easier to read. I'm terrible at being concise, and always use more words than needed (as the editors of this book will attest!). I've found that Twitter is a great place to practice concise writing—I often rewrite tweets again and again to make them fit inside the character restriction.

Terminology can be hard to get right. Usually it's best to avoid being too technical. What are the chances that the average person on the street even knows what a "browser" is? Some don't even consider the name of the app they're using, but focus on the job it does: "I use the web program" or "I use the internet button."

Similarly, jargon should be avoided. Have you ever had a conversation with someone who uses an acronym for every other word? If the reader isn't familiar with the meaning of the acronym or abbreviation, they can lose any understanding of the text: "Please get this GRN to AP ASAP for the COO."

In other contexts, acronyms can be okay—even necessary. For example, if you started talking about "Hypertext Markup Language and Cascading Style Sheets," fewer web industry folks would understand you than if you said "HTML and CSS." Just in case, it's best to include the meaning of the acronym or abbreviation the first time you use it on a page: "We make websites using Hypertext Markup Language (HTML) and Cascading Style Sheets (CSS). HTML gives our content structure; CSS gives it style."

Using vague terms with unclear meaning creates similar problems. "Blue-sky thinking" is the kind of language that conjures up awful business stock photos. When in doubt, say something as plainly as possible. "Creative thinking" makes you sound less foolish anyway.

TYPOGRAPHY

Once you have a visual hierarchy in place, with headings, paragraphs, lists, and emphases, you can use typography to further enhance the readability of the text. Accessibility lies in keeping the text as legible as possible—and the font family, size, and line height you choose has an impact.

- Font size: If small text can be hard to read, overly big text can pose problems, too, forcing you to sit back to be able to read at a comfortable distance. Ample font sizes help as many people as possible read your text. The generally recommended font size is the equivalent of 16 pixels or larger, but this of course depends on the font.
- Font weight: Thin type became more popular when high-resolution screens became more prevalent. But thin type can be hard to read as it has a lower contrast against the background than heavier type does. It's also rendered very differently on standard and high-resolution displays—it loses clarity at standard resolution—so it's important to take care when using it, particularly at small sizes.

- Line length: Text crowded on to a short line length can be difficult to read because the text is broken up into such small groups. When a line is longer than about 66 characters (http://webtypography.net/2.1.2), you can find yourself having to turn your head from side to side to read the text, or getting sore eyes. Finding a balanced line length will make a big difference to people with difficulty reading.

Jason Santa Maria's *On Web Typography* (http://bkaprt.com/afe/04-04/) and Richard Rutter's recent *Web Typography* (http://bkaprt.com/afe/04-05/) both contain a wealth of information on choosing fonts and arranging type. As with general usability, thoughtful typography will benefit everyone.

Specialist typefaces

There are specialist typefaces designed to aid young readers and people who have difficulty reading. Heinemann is an unfussy typeface that uses the same shapes for characters as many people are taught to write in school: the *a*, for instance, has a single story and a large round counter (the white space in the center of the shape) (**FIG 4.18**). Its numeral *9* has a straight stem (or main stroke) rather than a curved stem, which some claim is more legible. The oft-maligned Comic Sans, looked down on by many designers, shares some of Heinemann's simple letterforms, and so is often favored for signs and displays in classrooms (**FIG 4.18**).

Icon fonts

Fonts have become widely used for icons too. However, icon fonts can cause problems for accessibility, depending on their implementation. If the icon is mapped to an unrecognized glyph in the HTML, a screen reader will just ignore it (**FIG 4.19**). Some icon fonts map icons to whole words, which can work very well if, for example, your house icon reads as "home" in the HTML (**FIG 4.20**).

FIG 4.18: Heinemann (left) and Comic Sans (right) both use the single-story *a*, but their *9*s are different. Heinemann favors *9* as it would be written by hand.

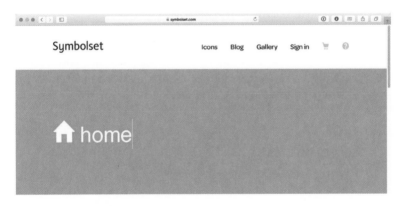

FIG 4.19: These buttons use an icon font for their arrow icons. VoiceOver doesn't recognize the `"\f061"` (arrow right) character and ignores it, but has no other content to read for this button.

FIG 4.20: Typing the word "home" in Symbolset results in a cute house icon (http://bkaprt.com/afe/04-06/).

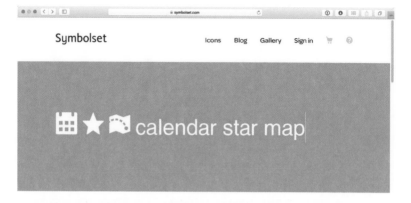

FIG 4.21: The icons in Symbolset are designed to use semantic and accessible terms but rely on you using the exact same term as they do.

However, these icon fonts rely on your using the symbols for the correct words in the font. Deciding to use the star symbol to mean "favorite" when the font uses it to mean "star" could result in screen readers uttering some odd-sounding language: "calendar, star, map" (**FIG 4.21**).

As with all frameworks and libraries, don't assume that because an icon font is widely-used, it's a best practice. If you choose to use icon fonts, be cautious to ensure you are not compromising accessibility. Use progressive enhancement so your icon fonts fall back to accessible text. (We'll look more at progressive enhancement in the next chapter.)

Font resizing

With the advent of mobile devices, readers often use the pinch gesture to zoom into text, making it bigger and easier to read on smaller screens. However, developers often disable zoom to gain greater control over the page layout resulting in an irritatingly common accessibility problem. To disable zoom, some developers use the viewport meta tag in the head element of their web pages:

```
<meta name="viewport" content="width=device-width,
  initial-scale=1.0, maximum-scale=1.0, user-
  scalable=no">
```

But if people find the text too small to read, using `user-scalable=no` and `maximum-scale=1.0` as options for the meta viewport could render your site inaccessible. You can safely leave these attributes out, and opt for the much cleaner:

```
<meta name="viewport" content="width=device-width,
  initial-scale=1.0">
```

INTERACTION DESIGN

People with learning difficulties and other cognitive impairments often find changes in content, following instructions, and entering an expected input challenging. Interfaces should allow users time to digest a page. When something goes wrong with an interaction, it should be easy to rectify any mistakes. If the page updates without user input, the changes should be identifiable and with a clear purpose.

Carousels and other animations often auto-advance content. Auto-advancing doesn't allow someone to finish reading content if they have difficulties, or if they're distracted. If you really must use a carousel, give visitors control over when the next slide advances. If you want to use a cool animation to aid somebody's understanding, make sure it's not so fast that it gets missed and not so slow that it gets in the way. Again, give users control so they can stop or skip animations.

When we require visitors to input content, we shouldn't allow the page to time-out without warning. If this is a security concern, give people the option to customize the timing to suit their needs. People should be allowed to take their time. Allow people to retrace their steps to review what they've entered earlier. This can help people who need to refresh their memory, particularly if they have cognitive impairments that can affect memory.

Forms

Forms are the key elements in interactive sites—they are, after all, how a user communicates with a site. But even filling out the shortest form can be taxing for people with learning difficulties. Form interactions should be made as stress-free as possible, assisting the user in filling out the form easily and accurately. People with literacy or language difficulties, for example, can benefit from spelling and grammar checks inside forms. Predictive text in search forms can assist people who have trouble spelling search terms correctly.

We've all been there: a form returns an error because what we've entered is in an "incorrect format," or the form field requires a specific format (**FIG 4.22**).

But that's not a user error—that's the site developers' fault. Formatting the content of an input field should not be a burden placed on the user; the burden should be on the developers to convert user input into the necessary format.

An input field should be constructed in a way that helps people enter the appropriate format. This could be through a JavaScript helper that converts their entry into the correct format on the fly (**FIG 4.23**), or even just microcopy clearly explaining the required format alongside the form field. (**FIG 4.24**). Asynchronous validation can also reassure people that their input is correct, resulting in a successful form submission.

If format conversion or asynchronous validation aren't possible, the contents of the form field should be converted after the form is submitted into the format needed by the site. That way the people using the site aren't unnecessarily challenged with working out the format required for their entries.

Alerts

Rich web applications have become more popular since the early 2000s, as the web has become more capable of providing interactive experiences. But rich web apps have introduced new accessibility issues: content on a page can change without being triggered by visitors. When an alert appears on a page without

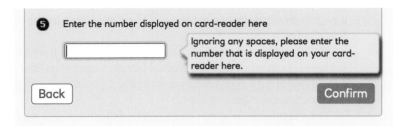

FIG 4.22: This text field has very specific information to "ignore any spaces." Why can't the form field remove my spaces if it knows that spaces are commonly entered?

FIG 4.23: Kickstarter's payment form checks if your card number is valid on the fly, making it harder for you to make a mistake.

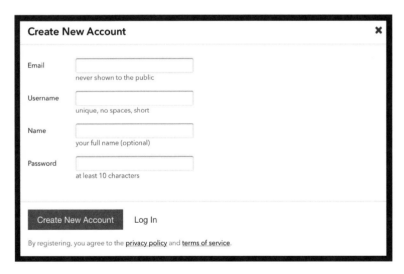

FIG 4.24: When you're creating a new account on a Discourse forum, there's helpful microcopy below each text input to give you some guidance.

a page refresh, visitors need to have their attention drawn to that change.

We often use contrasting boxes near the top of the viewport for alerts, instantly capturing sighted people's attention. However, those using screen readers also need a cue to tell them that the state has changed (**FIG 4.25**).

The alert should be given focus, alerting the user to the state change. Twitter does this very well. When a person using a screen reader views a Twitter feed, an instant alert announces: "New tweets available. Press period to review them." The Twitter alert doesn't just give you the changed state, but also gives you a keyboard shortcut to access those changes (**FIG 4.26**).

Once people have interacted with an alert, they should be able to return to their original position on the page.

Error messages

There are many different types of error messages: error messages on forms as the result of an interaction gone wrong; or even a simple "Page Not Found." Error messages can either fix a problem, or confuse and frustrate us. These little chunks of text attract visitors' attention, so making sure that the copy is friendly, appropriate, and useful is effort well spent (**FIG 4.27**).

Sometimes these snippets of text are written by developers who are just passing on the error from the server, forgetting that there's a human being on the other side (**FIG 4.28**).

If the user has done something wrong, explain clearly how they can rectify or get around the error (**FIG 4.29**).

Everyone on the team is responsible for creating a good experience for the people visiting their site. "Human copy" goes a long way in helping someone understand a problem, and how to fix it.

FIG 4.25: Twitter uses an alert bar above your Twitter feed to visually notify you of new Tweets.

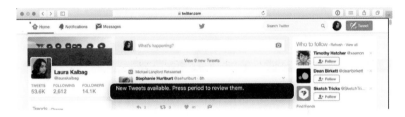

FIG 4.26: Twitter uses Accessible Rich Internet Applications (ARIA) to announce new Tweets to screen readers, so you're not excluded if you cannot see the visual alert. We'll look at ARIA more in the next chapter.

FIG 4.27: What's worse than a vague error message? No error message! This form doesn't even explain why my email address is formatted incorrectly, it just subtly turns the bottom border and icon red.

FIG 4.28: When this error came up on the Estée Lauder site, I wasn't sure if I'd done something wrong or was just on the receiving end of a peculiar log message.

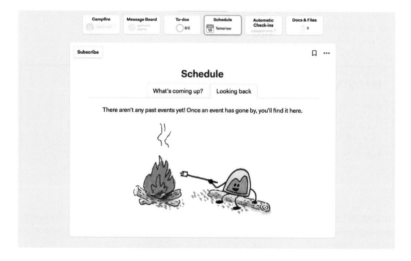

FIG 4.29: There are no past events in my Schedule, but instead of showing an error or an empty page, Basecamp tells me how this feature works, with a bonus cute illustration.

COLOR

In Chapter 2, we learned about how different types of color blindness affect how people perceive colors on sites. But color is more than a decorative choice; we use color to create a particular atmosphere or draw attention to specific elements on a page. In different cultures, colors may also take on different meanings, such as those associated with political parties or gender stereotypes. Color is never an arbitrary choice, and can easily be the downfall or success of your accessible design.

Contrast

Text whose color is too close to that of the background will be hard to read. Someone with a visual impairment will find this scenario particularly difficult, but all readers struggle with low-contrast text, especially if they're using old displays or sitting in bright sunlight. High contrast can help make a screen easier to read in such situations (**FIG 4.30**).

Low contrast isn't just a problem on plain backgrounds—contrast issues can also occur when text is on a textured background or on top of an image (**FIG 4.31**). Sufficient contrast between foreground and background colors makes text much easier to read. People who are color-blind are particularly affected by low color contrast, since they find it difficult to distinguish between colors.

To some degree, using big or bold type will make your text stand out from the background. This frees you up to use slightly lower-contrast colors since the size and weight of the type will do some of the work of distinguishing text from background.

While we aim for high contrast for the majority of visitors, if the contrast between text and background is too high, the text can appear to dance on screen. High-contrast text is particularly problematic for people with a dyslexic condition called *scotopic sensitivity syndrome* (SSS). People with SSS find that high-contrast text appears to shimmer or wobble on the screen.

FIG 4.30: These two color schemes may be similar, but the low contrast version (left) is much harder to read than the high contrast version (right).

FIG 4.31: When text is used over a photo with different textures and shapes in the background (left), the text is much harder to read and appears lower in contrast than against a solid color background (right).

Geri Coady, author of the fantastic *Color Accessibility Workflows*, recommends working in grayscale to test your designs. In grayscale, you can quickly see whether the text is readable against the background (**FIG 4.32**).

Till the Clouds Roll By (PG) ★ ★ ★ ★ ★
1947

Till the Clouds Roll By (PG)
1947

FIG 4.32: The design in color (upper) looks fairly high contrast, but when you see it in greyscale (lower), you can see the pink stars disappear into the blue background.

Avoiding contrast that is either too low or too high can feel like a difficult balancing act. Use your best judgment. And back it up with color-contrast checking tools and color-blindness emulation tools, which we'll discuss in Chapter 6.

Color as information

Color should never be used as the sole means of conveying information. On ecommerce sites, we're often given a choice between different colors for a product. On the Body Shop's site, for example, color choices are displayed as little colored squares. However, no text equivalent is provided unless you select the color swatch first. Without supplemental text, the little colored squares are meaningless to people who are visually impaired or color-blind (**FIG 4.33**).

Using both the color swatch and the color name on product pages gives the user a fallback. It also makes the page accessible if the images don't load.

Red is often used in forms to distinguish required fields or error fields because it's a bright and eye-catching color. However, to many color-blind and visually impaired users, red is indistinguishable—so a form with errors will look the same as a form without errors. Users with cognitive difficulties or little previous experience on the web may also find it hard to understand (**FIG 4.34**).

FIG 4.33: Fashionable names for colors can be unhelpful too. A nail polish in Relish The Moment may appear pickle green for someone with deuteranopia color blindness (simulated right) compared to its actual red (left).

FIG 4.34: The form errors on Etsy have a pink-red highlighted background, which is still very noticeable when you see the same form in grayscale.

Visual styling is still a valuable tool for getting the visitor's attention, but using text explanations in addition to red borders will make an error or required field accessible to as many people as possible.

RICH MEDIA

Images are the most popular form of rich media on the web. Many people with learning disabilities or low literacy benefit from content that uses images to support the text. I don't mean stock photos of people in suits high fiving, I mean photos and illustrations that aid the reader's understanding. Simple diagrams can also be very useful, as people who struggle to read may find it easier to understand information when it's presented visually.

Alt text

The `img` element allows us to embed images in web pages. The `alt` (short for "alternative") text attribute provides a text alternative to the image, which is shown to people if the image doesn't load, or if they're using a screen reader, which can't read images.

When we add the `alt` attribute to HTML, we're providing visitors with an alternative to content they may not be able to consume. If images haven't loaded or have been disabled, a sighted user will see the alt text, a screen reader will read the alt text, and a search engine will index the alt text. We can add alt text to our HTML like this:

```
<img src="DSCF0017.jpg" alt="the most adorable husky
   puppy you ever did see"/>
```

When a screen reader comes across an image that has no `alt` attribute, in an attempt to provide some useful information, it will sometimes read the file name instead. Not surprisingly, when images have digital file names like photo.jpg or DSCF0017.jpg, that's not very useful at all.

Providing text alternatives for images can help someone understand the context of an image without seeing the image itself. We don't need to be overly descriptive. Poor alternative text for an image might be something like "a dog in the park." But describing the image as "My dog Oskar sitting by a *hun-*

FIG 4.35: The key information about this photo is that a dog is sitting by a sign. The sign is unusual, so what it says is important.

drastplats sign which means 'dog park' in Swedish" gives more context and meaning to the image (**FIG 4.35**).

Alternative text is not necessary for a decorative image, as decoration is more about providing atmosphere than information. In these cases, we should still use the alternative attribute, but leave the contents of the attribute blank, to tell the browser and screen readers that this image is not important:

```
<img src="random-stock-photo.png alt="">
```

Simon Cox, senior consultant for global publishing services at HSBC bank, has found accessible alternative text to be a sticking point. Stakeholders sometimes want to use alt text as a space to hide search engine keywords. (Search engines can "see" the alt text just like screen readers can.) However, this provides an awful experience for screen readers. Imagine reading down a page of film posters, and instead of alt text you suddenly hear irrelevant keywords: "husky, malamute, dogs, parks, celebrities, stars, gossip, fashion, photos." Not cool.

Cox emphasizes that accessibility requirements should always trump search engine optimization: "Normally a good compromise can be found that meets accessibility requirements and will work well for SEO—then everybody is happy."

Text in images

Using images to present text was very popular before the days of webfonts, and unfortunately still persists occasionally to this day. However, text in JGPs, GIFs, and PNGs can't be resized and, if zoomed, becomes pixelated and harder to read. It also can't be read by screen readers, search engines, or autotranslators, and any revisions to the text become much more labor-intensive. In short, it's a terrible idea.

It's only worth putting text in an image if it's part of a logo. That's the only realistic use case nowadays. With the wide support of Scalable Vector Graphics (SVG), we can also include scalable and stylable text in SVGs, which is a simple way to make graphics more accessible. See Chris Coyier's *Practical SVG* on how best to use SVG text (http://bkaprt.com/afe/04-07/).

Graphs and infographics

Graphs and infographics are a great way to make information easy to digest; they can tell stories and make connections in an engaging way (**FIG 4.36**). Providing text alternatives to explain the content is usually the most straightforward method of approaching screen reader accessibility (**FIG 4.37**).

Some ways of going about this are more intelligent than others, though. Simply dumping the words of an infographic into a paragraph won't be very enlightening for readers, and neither will spitting out all the data from a graph. After all, we use graphs and infographics to make it easier to understand data—presenting that data as a chunk of obscure text defeats the point. It might help to think about how you would explain the contents of the media to someone over the phone, or via email. Ask yourself: what are the highlights and lowlights of

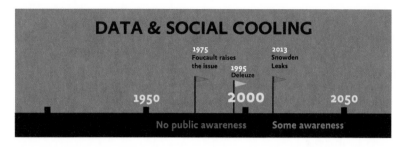

FIG 4.36: An infographic showing how public awareness of social cooling has increased since the Snowden leaks in 2013. (Infographic reproduced courtesy of Tijmen Schep, http://bkaprt.com/afe/04-08/.)

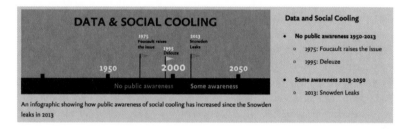

FIG 4.37: The same infographic with the contents simply described alongside, making it more accessible for everyone.

the infographic you're describing? What are its important and notable parts?

A text alternative may also be of use to someone who, because of cognitive or learning challenges, has difficulty understanding data presented in graphs and infographics. Furthermore, a text alternative offers a backup for all users, in case the image hasn't loaded or the graphing library isn't supported.

PDFs

When we're using the web, we expect content to be provided in a format that can be consumed on the web. Sites that offer content in PDFs, however, are dashing all those hopes and expectations.

Links to PDFs have inconsistent behaviors. Some web browsers will display the PDF in the browser window, but many will download the PDF to be opened and read by software on the device's operating system. The change of context breaks the flow, and makes it much harder for the user to regain their place in the website.

And PDFs themselves aren't accessible. As they're a proprietary format created by Adobe, not everyone can open and read PDFs without downloading additional software. They also take a lot more time and effort to make them readable by search engines and screen readers—at least HTML can be read by default.

Instead of using PDFs to provide content, recreate the content using HTML. It will be easier to find, easier to read, and a lot more accessible. If you need your content to be suitable for printing, consider print stylesheets that instruct the browser how best to style each HTML page when printed. Smashing Magazine (http://bkaprt.com/afe/04-09/) and CSS-Tricks (http://bkaprt.com/afe/04-10/) both have good articles on creating print stylesheets.

Tools that produce HTML from PDFs are also an option if your organization has loads of PDFs that need to be put online in a more accessible format. A quick web search will reveal plenty of PDF-to-HTML conversion tools. You don't need a tool that perfectly reproduces the PDF, as long as the conversion outputs usable HTML that can be slotted into your existing page templates.

Transcripts

When it comes to audio and video content, the easiest way to make it available to a wider audience is through transcripts. Transcripts are a text equivalent of speech and are usually less expensive and time-consuming to create than subtitles, closed captions, and sign-language interpretation.

Transcripts are useful to a wide range of people confronting any number of scenarios:

- hearing impairments
- difficulty cognitively processing audio
- non-native familiarity with the audio language
- noisy environments that make listening difficult
- quiet environments that make audio disruptive
- low bandwidth, which can cause make downloading audio and video to be slow and/or expensive

Personally, I prefer transcripts to videos; I find I concentrate better when reading than when listening. Skimming a transcript is much easier than skipping through a video to try to find the information you want.

The least expensive way to produce a transcript is to transcribe the text yourself. This can be a slow and arduous process. When I've transcribed short videos, I've found that it usually takes four or five times as long as the video itself. Professional transcribers are much quicker and can therefore be very good value for money.

Then there's speech-to-text software, which can be used to dictate your transcript. However, such software works best in situations with only one speaker, since it usually relies on learning individual speech patterns.

When transcribing audio or video as text, it's helpful to indicate who is speaking, especially if there are multiple speakers:

Suzy: What do you think of this new lamp I bought?
Aneel: I think I prefer the one we have in the kitchen.

It's also good practice to include all of the relevant auditory and visual information in brackets to help the reader understand the context of the speech. Think of it like writing a script.

[Suzy is in the hall with Aneel, Emily and Jessica]
Suzy: What do you [Suzy points at Aneel] think of this new lamp I bought?
[Emily nods a sign of approval. Jessica looks at Aneel expectantly]
Aneel: I think I prefer the one we have in the kitchen.

Similarly, you may want to leave out irrelevant auditory and visual information to produce a *clean verbatim* transcript. "[Jessica coughs]" doesn't aid the understanding of the text. However, "ums", "ers" and other stutters and hesitations can offer more context and humanize a transcript. Including these details produces a *true verbatim* transcript, which is usually costlier than a clean verbatim transcript.

> [Annie looks at the food on Sam's plate]
> Annie: That looks... um... tasty.

There aren't any particular standards for formatting transcripts, and they work best as good old HTML. Rendering your transcript in well-structured HTML makes it easy to read and easy for search engines to find. I prefer to add headings and links to my transcripts as it makes them even easier to navigate and provides additional value over the audio or video.

Subtitles and captions

If you've watched a movie in a language that's foreign to you, you've probably seen subtitles. *Subtitles* are lines of text that are usually transcriptions or translations of what's being spoken on the screen. They appear at the same time as the spoken word, so you can understand the movie without speaking the same language.

Closed captions, on the other hand, provide the same information present in subtitles, but also include other audio cues, such as "[music]" to describe when music is the only sound, or "[doorbell rings]" when an important sound effect is heard. Only important audio cues that are pertinent to understanding the movie are included in closed captions. Having "[sirens in distant background]" in a scene set in New York wouldn't provide much meaningful detail when describing a city known for its loud traffic.

As with transcripts, there are professional services that will create closed captions for you, but as it's time-consuming work, these services can be expensive. YouTube has an auto-captioning option on videos, but speech-to-text software can be

appetizers are dealing with this
is where they get their data

Laura Kalbag: Ethical Design

6:49 / 18:49

FIG 4.38: YouTube's auto-captioning is good, though tastily replaced "advertisers" with "appetizers" throughout this talk I gave at Creative Mornings Malmö.

inaccurate if there is background noise, multiple speakers, or an accent unfamiliar to the software (**FIG 4.38**).

Producing your own closed captions will be the least expensive option and will enable you to write the most accurate text. Writing good closed captions is an art. You don't want to show too much text on the screen at any one time, as it makes it harder to read alongside the main picture (**FIG 4.39**).

Closed captions are most comfortably read in short bursts, since they are shown at exactly the same time as the speech and sound on screen. If there are pauses or silence in the speech, the captions can be shown for longer, giving readers more time to absorb the text. Full sentences are far too long, and the text shouldn't carry over into two lines unless your screen size is very small. If you watch closed captions on TV, or in a movie theater, you'll get an idea of the right line length and where it's comfortable to put a break in a phrase.

Both YouTube and Vimeo have functions for uploading your own closed-caption files, and you can create closed captions for YouTube inside their video editor. Whether you're rolling your

that's the insight that it sells to its customers.

02:21

own video player using HTML5 or using YouTube or Vimeo, you can use a Web Video Text Track (WebVTT) file (.vtt) for your captions.

A .vtt file is a simple text file that lists all of the text for the captions, with timestamps telling the text when to appear on screen. It can also include meta information such as a chapter list and description of the video, as well as simple styling and structuring markup.

```
WEBVTT
00:00:00.782 --> 00:00:05.000
Today, on Spyware 2.0: "Privacy"

00:00:05.100 --> 00:00:07.493
When we think of a private conversation,
```

```
00:00:07.593 --> 00:00:10.593
we think of it taking place between two people.

00:00:10.896 --> 00:00:12.380
And that's how it should be.

00:00:12.480 --> 00:00:14.547
Just between you and the person you're having

00:00:14.647 --> 00:00:16.715
the private conversation with.
```

The .vtt markup is simple and very readable, but it takes a lot of time to work out the correct timestamps to mark up each caption. There are a few free apps (see Resources) that help you create captions. These tend to work with an audio or video file, and provide an interface that makes it easy to add and edit captions while hearing or watching the audio or video playing.

A GENEROUS USER EXPERIENCE

Designing user experiences often means making assumptions about users' preferences. While we should question those assumptions, and use research to better inform ourselves about user preferences, sometimes just providing a different way, an alternative, can make a huge difference. Alternatives allow someone to choose whichever way works best for them.

Even when people have an impairment that could benefit from an assistive technology, we should never assume that they're using an assistive technology. Maybe their disability isn't severe enough to benefit from assistive-technology support. Maybe technologies that could help them, such as screen readers and custom input mechanisms, are too expensive. Maybe they aren't even aware that technologies that could help them access the web exist. Sometimes, too, people have a secondary impairment, and use technology specific to another need.

Some people rely on alternative ways of consuming content, while others simply prefer certain formats. I'm not a fan of watching long videos of conference talks; I'd far rather skim through a transcript with pictures of the slides to find the bits that interest me the most. I'm not suggesting that we should provide several different versions and formats of our sites to please everyone, but providing alternatives for accessibility reasons has the side benefit of working for a much wider audience.

We can make small, thoughtful changes to our websites. We can be generous with our design. We can make great, rather than just adequate, experiences.

Now that we have a good foundation in making usable interfaces, we can look at *how* to mark up those interfaces, giving them structure and meaning that is accessible in the browser.

5 ACCESSIBILITY AND HTML

THE PRIMARY ROLE OF the browser in web accessibility is to connect HTML to the accessibility layer of the operating system. To achieve that, browser makers follow the Accessibility API Mapping standards so that their browsers correctly interpret our markup, and we follow web standards so that our markup is correctly interpreted by browsers.

This means that when we write well-structured HTML, without altering the default behaviors, it is innately accessible. It's that easy—job done. You can go home now.

Well-structured HTML is the secret weapon of web accessibility. With a solid HTML foundation, a site becomes instantly more accessible to a much wider audience.

THE IMPORTANCE OF STRUCTURE

HTML is simple and easy to read because its basic job is to provide structure to a web page's content. It's mostly just content surrounded with element tags. Many of us don't bother thinking or learning about HTML elements in depth, as they just seem so straightforward. But there's a lot of accessibility goodness to master in the default behavior of HTML elements, and this makes them worth taking the time to understand.

View the bare HTML structure of any web page by removing its CSS styles. You can do this using any modern web browser:

- Firefox: Go to View > Page Styles > No Style.
- Safari: Enable Developer Tools in Preferences > Advanced > Checkbox for "Show Develop menu in menu bar". Then from the Develop menu, select Disable Styles.
- Internet Explorer: Go to Command Bar > Page > Style > No Style.
- Opera and Chrome (also works for Firefox and Safari): Download Chris Pederick's Web Developer extension (http://bkaprt.com/afe/05-01/). Then from the Web Developer extension, go to CSS > Disable CSS.

Unstyled HTML looks slightly different in each browser because it uses the browser's default styles. These default styles vary depending on the combination of the browser and the operating system. When we write CSS, we override the browser's default styles with our own.

A unstyled view of an HTML document approximates the way it would be read by a screen reader—from top to bottom. If the most important information on a page is at the bottom, most visitors will skim and skip and scroll to get to the good stuff. But screen readers can't skim for patterns and context, so it's crucial that the content is in an order that make sense to the screen reader, with the most important information appearing first (**FIG 5.1**).

Books usually have tables of contents to give the book structure and show the reader what's to come. In the same way, screen readers benefit from headings and other structural HTML elements that create a content outline for a web page (**FIG 5.2**).

An accessible content structure also gives search engines something to grab onto, making content easier for people to find.

FIG 5.1: The unstyled HTML for the Wikipedia page about huskies looks unexciting, but the content is all there.

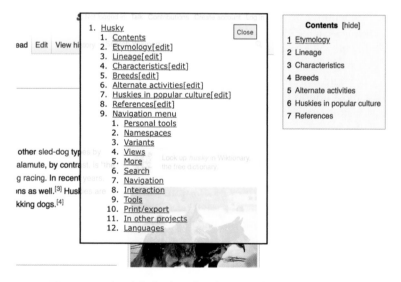

FIG 5.2: The HTML outline (left) for the Wikipedia page on huskies is reflected in its Contents page navigation (right)

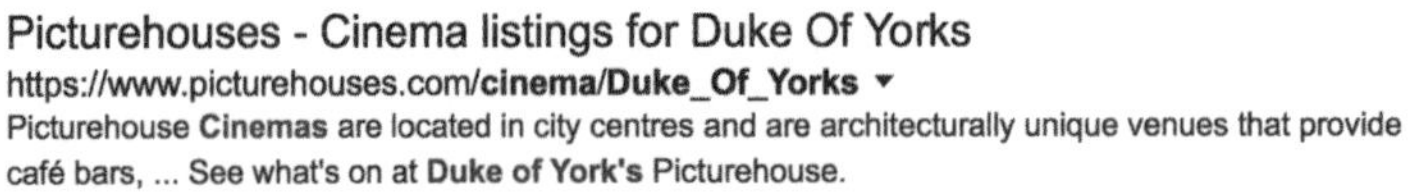

Picturehouses - Cinema listings for Duke Of Yorks
https://www.picturehouses.com/**cinema/Duke_Of_Yorks** ▾
Picturehouse **Cinemas** are located in city centres and are architecturally unique venues that provide
café bars, ... See what's on at **Duke of York's** Picturehouse.

FIG 5.3: Google uses the `<title>` for the result heading, then `<meta description>` and
the page's first `<h1>` as the result description.

Findability

Search engines rely on crawlers that index websites for content,
then use algorithms to determine the relevance of that content
to search keywords. Good accessibility increases findability
because it benefits search engine optimization. Search engine
crawlers behave much like screen readers: they can't easily or
intelligently understand images, audio, or video, so they benefit
from text alternatives and well-written content.

If you look at Google's design and content guidelines, they're
exactly the same as the suggestions you'd find in accessibility
guidelines (http://bkaprt.com/afe/05-02/):

> *"Create a useful, information-rich site, and write pages that
> clearly and accurately describe your content."*
> *"Think about the words users would type to find your pages,
> and make sure that your site actually includes those words
> within it."*
> *"Design your site to have a clear conceptual page hierarchy."*

A clear site structure and hierarchy allows search engines to
better understand what the most valuable content is on your
site, and what would make up a valuable preview in search
results. If you look at some typical Google (**FIG 5.3**) and Duck-
DuckGo (**FIG 5.4**) search results, you can see how each search
engine uses the page title element for the main title of the
result. They then use the first h1 and h2 elements to give you a
rough idea of the content on that page.

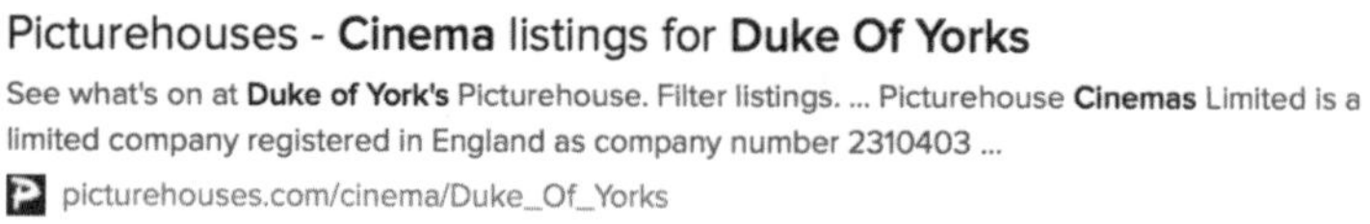

Picturehouses - **Cinema** listings for **Duke Of Yorks**

See what's on at **Duke of York's** Picturehouse. Filter listings. ... Picturehouse **Cinemas** Limited is a limited company registered in England as company number 2310403 ...

P picturehouses.com/cinema/Duke_Of_Yorks

FIG 5.4: DuckDuckGo uses the page's `<title>` for the result heading, then the first `<h1>` and a `<p>` from near the end of the page as the result description.

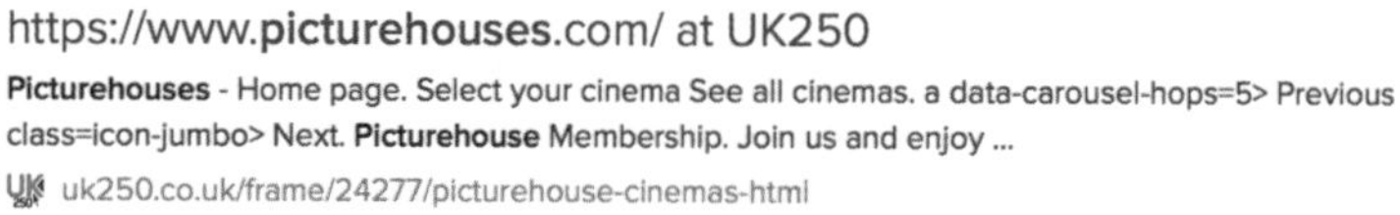

https://www.**picturehouses**.com/ at UK250

Picturehouses - Home page. Select your cinema See all cinemas. a data-carousel-hops=5> Previous class=icon-jumbo> Next. **Picturehouse** Membership. Join us and enjoy ...

UK uk250.co.uk/frame/24277/picturehouse-cinemas-html

FIG 5.5: This search result looks like an automatically generated page. It doesn't have a meaningful title, and somehow bits of HTML show up in the description.

When a page's HTML isn't structured clearly, it can have a negative effect on the search results preview (**FIG 5.5**). It's much harder to identify the type of content you'd find on that page, so it's less likely to come up in relevant search engine results.

Headings

In order to create a meaningful content outline, we need to use headings to create a structure (**FIG 5.6**). There is an argument that in HTML5 we can use more than one h1 element on a page, but browsers have better support when we use a singular h1 to title or describe the main function of a page.

h2 elements describe second-level headings. There is often more than one h2 element on a page. h3, h4, h5, and h6 headings can be used to break content down even further. These elements tend to be seen less often, but the content outline for a highly-structured page (like a typical Wikipedia entry) reveals multiple heading levels in use.

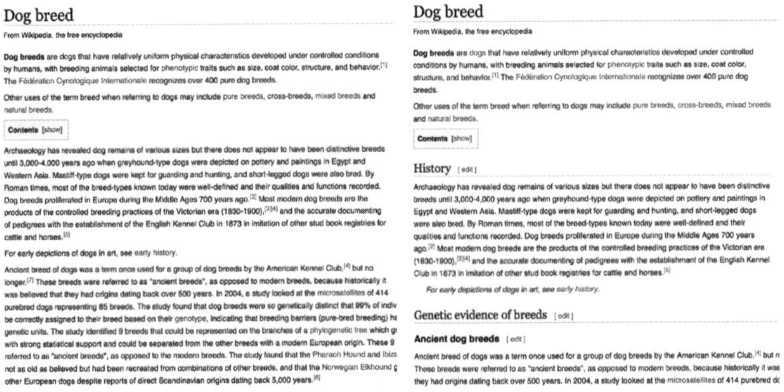

Dog breed

From Wikipedia, the free encyclopedia

Dog breeds are dogs that have relatively uniform physical characteristics developed under controlled conditions by humans, with breeding animals selected for phenotypic traits such as size, coat color, structure, and behavior.[1] The Fédération Cynologique Internationale recognizes over 400 pure dog breeds.

Other uses of the term breed when referring to dogs may include pure breeds, cross-breeds, mixed breeds and natural breeds.

Contents [show]

Archaeology has revealed dog remains of various sizes but there does not appear to have been distinctive breeds until 3,000-4,000 years ago when greyhound-type dogs were depicted on pottery and paintings in Egypt and Western Asia. Mastiff-type dogs were kept for guarding and hunting, and short-legged dogs were also bred. By Roman times, most of the breed-types known today were well-defined and their qualities and functions recorded. Dog breeds proliferated in Europe during the Middle Ages 700 years ago.[2] Most modern dog breeds are the products of the controlled breeding practices of the Victorian era (1830-1900),[3][4] and the accurate documenting of pedigrees with the establishment of the English Kennel Club in 1873 in imitation of other stud book registries for cattle and horses.[5]

For early depictions of dogs in art, see early history.

Ancient breed of dogs was a term once used for a group of dog breeds by the American Kennel Club,[4] but no longer.[7] These breeds were referred to as "ancient breeds", as opposed to modern breeds, because historically it was believed that they had origins dating back over 500 years. In 2004, a study looked at the microsatellites of 414 purebred dogs representing 85 breeds. The study found that dog breeds were so genetically distinct that 99% of indiv be correctly assigned to their breed based on their genotype, indicating that breeding barriers (pure-bred breeding) ha genetic units. The study identified 9 breeds that could be represented on the branches of a phylogenetic tree which gr with strong statistical support and could be separated from the other breeds with a modern European origin. These 9 referred to as "ancient breeds", as opposed to the modern breeds. The study found that the Pharaoh Hound and Ibiza not as old as believed but had been recreated from combinations of other breeds, and that the Norwegian Elkhound g other European dogs despite reports of direct Scandinavian origins dating back 5,000 years.[6]

Dog breed

From Wikipedia, the free encyclopedia

Dog breeds are dogs that have relatively uniform physical characteristics developed under controlled conditions by humans, with breeding animals selected for phenotypic traits such as size, coat color, structure, and behavior.[1] The Fédération Cynologique Internationale recognizes over 400 pure dog breeds.

Other uses of the term breed when referring to dogs may include pure breeds, cross-breeds, mixed breeds and natural breeds.

Contents [show]

History [edit]

Archaeology has revealed dog remains of various sizes but there does not appear to have been distinctive breeds until 3,000-4,000 years ago when greyhound-type dogs were depicted on pottery and paintings in Egypt and Western Asia. Mastiff-type dogs were kept for guarding and hunting, and short-legged dogs were also bred. By Roman times, most of the breed-types known today were well-defined and their qualities and functions recorded. Dog breeds proliferated in Europe during the Middle Ages 700 years ago.[2] Most modern dog breeds are the products of the controlled breeding practices of the Victorian era (1830-1900),[3][4] and the accurate documenting of pedigrees with the establishment of the English Kennel Club in 1873 in imitation of other stud book registries for cattle and horses.[5]

For early depictions of dogs in art, see early history.

Genetic evidence of breeds [edit]

Ancient dog breeds [edit]

Ancient breed of dogs was a term once used for a group of dog breeds by the American Kennel Club,[4] but n These breeds were referred to as "ancient breeds", as opposed to modern breeds, because historically it was they had origins dating back over 500 years. In 2004, a study looked at the microsatellites of 414 purebred dc

FIG 5.6: Without headings to structure the content, a Wikipedia page would look intimidating, and would be hard to skim (left). It's good that the real Wikipedia uses headings to make long pages of content easier to read and reference (right).

If the text lacked hierarchy, it would take a lot longer for readers to skim, to understand what the page was about, or to locate a particular piece of information.

Lists

Lists are another way of breaking up body text into a meaningful structure. Lists break up text into bite-sized chunks, and it's easy for screen readers and keyboard shortcuts to skip from one list item to the next just by reading the first few words.

The `ul` element is used for unordered lists, where the order of the list items isn't really important. By default, browsers show `ul` list items with bullet points. The `ol` element is used for ordered lists, where a strict order is integral to the list—by default, browsers will number `ol` list items. Screen readers will usually read the numbers or say "bullet" at the beginning of each list item, even if the numbers or bullet points have been removed or hidden by the CSS styles.

FORMS

Sometimes developers add JavaScript to a `span` or `div` element to make it interactive, and to mimic the behavior of a true interactive element like a button or an input. They do this to give themselves more control over the default appearance and behavior of an element. But this is a misuse of `spans` and `divs`. Not only will you lose the default accessibility benefits you'd get from the interactive elements, you can also waste a lot of time trying to recreate similar behavior and styles.

Incredibly rich interaction can be created through buttons and inputs, no JavaScript needed. Let's take a look at some of the most important form elements and the default interactive behavior the browser provides for each.

Inputs

Different input elements—like text fields, dropdown selectors, radio buttons, and checkboxes—help people enter information into forms in different ways .

All of these input types come with default accessibility features that allow a screen reader to read the state of the input. For example, when someone selects a radio button that has already been selected, the screen reader reads "selected, radio button". If the radio button is unselected, the screen reader just says "radio button".

Labels

Without labels, input fields are useless. Labels describe the expected input. Similar to navigation labels, input labels should be clear and concise, explaining to the user exactly what's expected. They should come before the input field in the HTML, so it's clear which label is associated with which form field. Labels for radio buttons and checkboxes are also accessible when they come after the input in the HTML. The visual placement of the labels is also important for the user to understand the expected input (**FIG 5.8**).

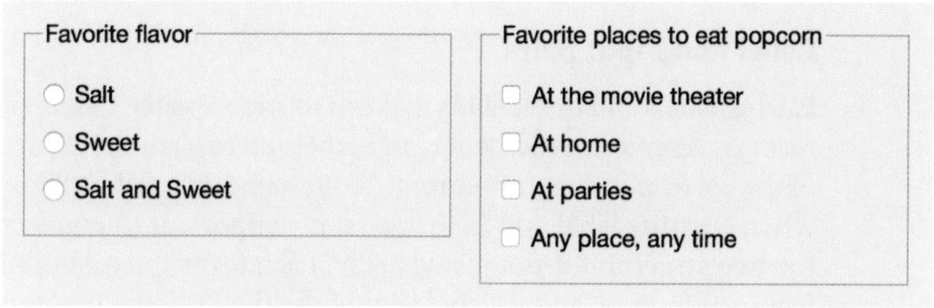

FIG 5.7: A text field label (such as "name" above) conventionally appears before or alongside the input box. Labels for radio buttons and checkboxes (such as "Salt" or "At the movie theater") always appear close alongside the input so the relationship between label and input is clear.

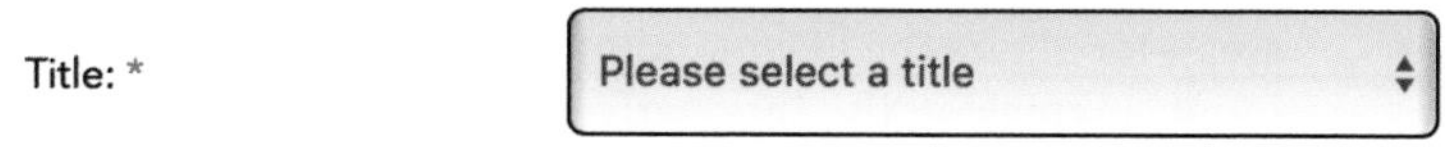

FIG 5.8: It's a tiny little star, how did it end up meaning "required"?

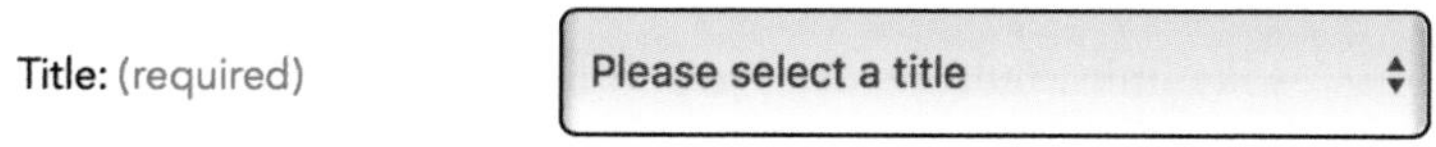

FIG 5.9: Adding "(required)" tells you exactly what you need to know. Also, titles are never a real requirement...

If the input field is required before a form can be submitted, the label should tell the user that. Often an asterisk is used to suggest a required field in a form, but this is a visual cue that only makes sense to users who have interacted with similar forms in the past (**FIG 5.8**).

The clearest way to show that a form field needs to be filled in is to clearly show the word "required" inside the label, alongside the name of the form field (**FIG 5.9**). This ensures there's no confusion for sighted or screen reader users, for people who are seasoned fillers of forms, or for first-time web users.

Label and input pairs

Pairing labels and input fields makes a form accessible to screen readers. A screen reader will read a label and explain the nature of the corresponding form input: "Your name, text field." Thus, when creating label and input pairs, it's important to connect the two structurally, not just visually. Each form `input` should have a unique `id`, and its label should use the `id` of the input in its `for=` attribute. This literally tells the browser which input field the label is for.

Pairing has other usability benefits, too. Most browsers will give focus to, or select, a form input when the user interacts with the label for that field (**FIG 5.10**). This is very useful when form inputs such as radio buttons have a small interactive area—it reduces the likelihood of the user selecting the wrong input. Increasing the interactive area aids people who have motor difficulties or are using a touchscreen, where using a cursor accurately can be challenging.

Buttons

Like links, buttons can have different states: inactive, active, hover, focus, and disabled (**FIG 5.11**). They can also have default types of interaction: a submit button tells the browser to submit the contents of a form, while a reset button tells the browser to clear the contents of a form.

When we're overriding these default styles with our own styles, we need to make sure we don't lose the interactive styles that visually describe the button states (**FIG 5.12**). Disabled buttons are generally not recommended as they rely on the user's understanding of the "disabled" visual style. Find out more about the usability issues with disabled buttons in the Resources section.

 Salt

FIG 5.10: As the `label` is paired with the radio button, and its style is set to `inline-block`, clicking or tapping anywhere in the dotted area will select the corresponding radio button.

FIG 5.11: Browsers provide default styles for buttons to make it clear that they're interactive. Using the `disabled` attribute makes a button appear visually disabled in a grayed-out style (right), as well as letting assistive technology know it is functionally disabled.

FIG 5.12: Even though the buttons have custom styles and colors, their different states are easy to distinguish.

KEYBOARD NAVIGATION

Keyboard navigation can be tricky if a site's developers have built features without keyboard access. Writing well-structured HTML with meaningful elements is the best possible foundation. Forms, dropdown menus, navigation, video, and audio are particularly hard for people relying on a keyboard to access—for instance, dropdown menus and navigation can be very fiddly if you need to use a mouse to hover a menu open *and* move to select the desired item at the same time.

Keyboard shortcuts

Although keyboard shortcuts can be useful for people relying on keyboard navigation, they have pitfalls. To return to Sam's experience, his cerebral palsy has made him "left-sided," meaning that he performs almost all his actions with his left hand, and switching contexts between a mouse and a keyboard is difficult. Sam mostly uses one finger to type, which makes his typing staccato, and makes reaching for shortcut key combinations (or even switching between uppercase and lowercase characters) difficult.

With rich applications becoming more popular, some web apps are using text shortcuts to mimic the experience of a native app. For example, you can find a list of text shortcuts on Twitter by selecting Shift-? on twitter.com (**FIG 5.13**).

Twitter shortcuts are of great value to some people using screen readers. When new tweets are available in the timeline, focus moves to a notification that informs the user: "New tweets available. Press Period to review them." The user doesn't have to navigate to the tweets area, but can instead just use the Period key.

As useful as these shortcuts are, keyboard shortcuts provided by JavaScript don't currently work with Windows screen readers. However, there is a hack to get around the problem, and support could be improved in the future. Read Léonie Watson's post "Time to revisit accesskey?" for a more in-depth explanation (http://bkaprt.com/afe/05-03/).

Access keys

Access keys went through a popular phase in the late 90s and early 00s, when developers created their own keyboard shortcuts for links on their sites using the accesskey HTML attribute. Often the navigation would show an underlined letter in the link text to inform the user of the access key shortcut, in a similar way to old Windows menus (**FIG 5.14**).

However, the modifier key for shortcuts varied across operating systems, and the access key modifiers (the key you hold down at the same time as the shortcut key) varied from browser

FIG 5.13: Twitter's "Keyboard shortcuts" use single-key shortcuts, which could make Sam's experience much better.

FIG 5.14: The Firefox toolbar in Windows 2000, showing F, E, V, G, B, T and H as shortcuts. Photograph courtesy Chris Waigl, (http://bkaprt.com/afe/05-04/).

to browser. As a result, access keys were confusing to document and use—in other words, not very accessible. We should bear this in mind if we create text shortcuts for our own sites, and not repeat the same mistakes we made in the past.

Skip links

Many sites use skip links to assist people using keyboard navigation. *Skip links* are a common accessibility feature allowing people to skip past lengthy navigation and go straight to the page content (**FIG 5.15**). They've also become a common form of navigation used on one-page sites that have a lot of content to scroll through.

Blog

Skip to search, categories and tags

FIG 5.15: I use a skip link on my blog's list page, so readers can get to the search, categories and tags section without having to scroll past all the blog posts I've ever written.

Some sites choose to make skip links invisible unless you're using a screen reader, but screen reader users rarely use skip links because screen readers have more sophisticated navigation to skip to content. Hiding skip links from everyone except screen reader users excludes the people who may benefit the most from skip links—sighted people using keyboard navigation. The best possible option is to make the skip links visible to all users so that all users benefit.

Keyboard focus and visual focus

Keyboard focus is the location on the page where the keyboard's actions are interpreted by the browser. If the keyboard focus is the same as the *visual focus (what you can see in the viewport)*, you'll be able to see what you type on the screen. If the keyboard focus is on a form field further down the page, but the visual focus is still stuck at the top of the page, you won't be able to see what you're typing on the screen.

Keyboard focus is particularly important to people who rely on the keyboard to navigate the web, since some browsers don't support skip links in HTML. At the time of writing, Safari and Chrome don't change the keyboard focus to the visual focus area when someone follows a skip link. This means you might be looking at the section you skipped to, but the keyboard focus is still on the navigation at the top of the page. If you tab to the next item, your visual focus will scroll right back to the top of the page.

FIG 5.16: Focus styles in Safari (left) and Firefox (right). Don't remove them. Or even better, replace the browser's default focus and hover styles with your own styles that both fit with your site's aesthetic and are even more visible.

The disjunction between visual and keyboard focus makes skip links utterly useless for keyboard navigation users as they're not actually skipping at all.

Focus and hover styles

Links, buttons, and inputs are given default interaction events and `tabindex` by the browser, and all are highlighted with *focus styles* by default. (We'll return to `tabindex` shortly.) When we move through these elements using keyboard navigation, the focus styles allow us to see where we are, and tell assistive technologies what to expect.

For people using keyboard navigation, focus styles (frequently displayed by browsers as a combination of dotted borders and blue glows) are indispensable. You might recognize these styles if you've removed them in the past when they didn't fit in with your site's aesthetic (**FIG 5.16**). (Don't worry, I won't tell anyone. Just go put them back now.)

Like focus styles, *hover styles* give us visual feedback as we navigate a page. Hover styles are most frequently used to show that we can interact with an element. Think about how links and buttons often change to a different color when we hover over them (**FIG 5.17**).

Because hover styles are most commonly used on interactive elements, they shouldn't be used on non-interactive elements. But at the same time, when designing hover styles, don't rely

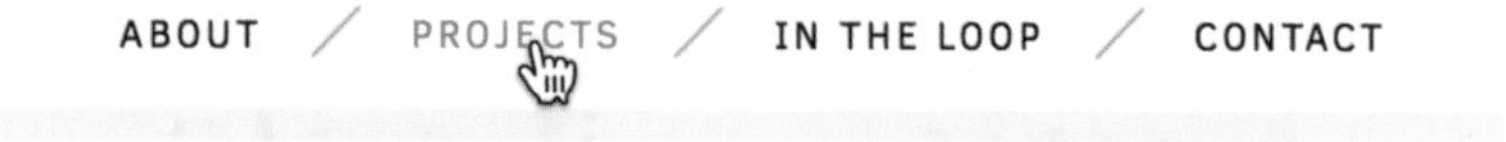

ABOUT / PROJECTS / IN THE LOOP / CONTACT

FIG 5.17: On the Tactical Tech site, the navigation link color changes on hover.

FIG 5.18: The hovering style on iOS can only be triggered by very lightly pressing a link.

on them for showing interaction. Not only are hover styles invisible to people with visual impairments, but they're also hidden from most touchscreen users—touchscreen devices rarely support the hover action (**FIG 5.18**).

If you make spans, divs, and other usually non-interactive elements into interactive elements, you create confusion for those using screen readers and keyboard navigation, which rely on the accessible cues provided by the default HTML. Keyboard navigation demands special consideration in rich applications, because events can change regularly on a page, causing confusion and disorientation if focus isn't managed correctly.

tabindex

HTML4 introduced the tabindex attribute, which describes the order of elements when navigated by keyboard (often done by pressing the Tab key). The standard tabindex is the order in which elements appear in the source code. If you want to make some elements appear in a different order to keyboard and screen reader users, you would use the `tabindex` attribute on the elements in question:

```
<ol>
    <li><a href="/" tabindex="1">Home</a></li>
    <li><a href="about.html" tabindex="3">About</
a></li>
    <li><a href="contact.html"
tabindex="2">Contact</a></li>
</ol>
```

But you shouldn't do this! If you did this, the tab order would be "Home, Contact, About." It would really confuse sighted people using keyboard navigation.

If a keyboard navigation user uses the Tab key to navigate, the `tabindex` order is honored, but if they use their cursor keys to navigate, the `tabindex` order is ignored. Because of these inconsistencies, altering the tab index is generally not advisable.

`tabindex="0"` and `tabindex="-1"` have distinct functions. `tabindex="0"` tells the keyboard navigation to recognize an element in the standard tab order. This can be used to make a non-interactive element, such as a `p` or a `div`, into an element that can be reached with keyboard tabbing. But as I've just described with focus styles, turning non-interactive elements into interactive elements can flummox people using screen readers and keyboard navigation.

`tabindex="-1"` removes an element from the tab index. That way no one can tab to it but the element can still receive focus from a link or via JavaScript. Remember earlier when we looked at how skip links can be a problem if the keyboard focus doesn't match the visual focus? Scott Vinkle found that using `tabindex="-1"` on the element targeted by the skip link allows it to receive programmatic focus (http://bkaprt.com/afe/05-05/). When the user hits Tab again, the focus will follow the expected behavior and move to the next focusable element in the tab order.

`tabindex="-1"` can also be valuable for more complex interfaces that try to behave like a desktop application interface. For example, a menu widget may want to receive tab focus (and so

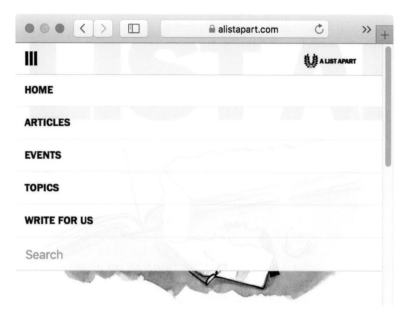

FIG 5.19: The A List Apart collapsible navigation menu is an example of a complex menu widget that you can navigate using only the keyboard.

uses `tabindex="0"`), but the list inside that menu may need to be controlled using Left and Right keys to expand and collapse the menu items. We can use `tabindex="-1"` to give the menu visual focus, but leave the keyboard focus control to JavaScript (**FIG 5.19**).

Although the `tabindex` attribute has its uses, it should never replace well-structured HTML: `tabindex` only affects keyboard navigation, not other input or output types.

SEPARATING STRUCTURE AND STYLE

If HTML is so accessible by default, then why aren't more sites accessible? There are many reasons why a site ends up with dodgy HTML, but the two main culprits I've seen are HTML

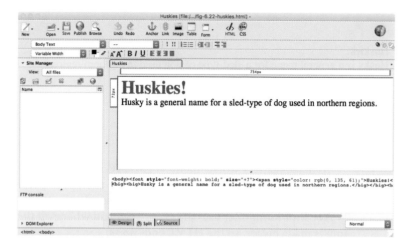

FIG 5.20: KompoZer, an old-school WYSIWYG editor, has a split view so you can preview your rendered HTML and CSS as you write.

generated from WYSIWYG editors and HTML elements used for their CSS styling.

WYSIWYG editors

What-You-See-Is-What-You-Get (WYSIWYG) editing software outputs HTML from content created in a visual editing interface. Although they've improved enormously over the last ten years, WYSIWYG editors can still be used to commit HTML atrocities. The problem with WYSIWYG editors lies in the name: they're designed to manipulate the appearance, not the structure, of the content. For example, if I wanted to make "Huskies!" into the title of my page, I would choose a big font size and a bright color to visually suggest its importance (**FIG 5.20**).

While making the text big and colorful makes it stand out to sighted users, it's completely meaningless to a screen reader or a search engine. When they read the unstyled HTML, all they see is another chunk of body text, exactly the same as the text around it (**FIG 5.21**).

Huskies!
Husky is a general name for a sled-type of dog used in northern regions.

To make matters worse, many WYSIWYG editors generate unnecessary elements and attributes in their attempt to parse meaning from visual design choices. For example, the WYSI-WYG editor KompoZer uses the `<font>` element whenever the font is made bigger, so the HTML ends up as:

```
<font style="font-weight: bold;" size="+7"><span
  style="color: rgb(0, 135, 61);">Huskies!</span></
  font>
<br>
<big><big>Husky is a general name for a sled-type of
  dog used in northern regions.</big></big>
<br>
```

`<font>` has been deprecated since HTML4. Don't be like KompoZer.

CSS styling

The same problem occurs when HTML elements are chosen because of their associated CSS style rather than because of their structural meaning.

Consider a bit of text that has a main title—"Huskies!"—and a subtitle—"Husky is a general name for a sled-type of dog used in northern regions." The hierarchy is very clear to sighted users (**FIG 5.22**).

When you look at the HTML and CSS, though, you see that the main title is in fact an h2 and the subtitle is an h1. They've only been chosen to mark up the content this way because of their visual presentation: the CSS has been written so that the

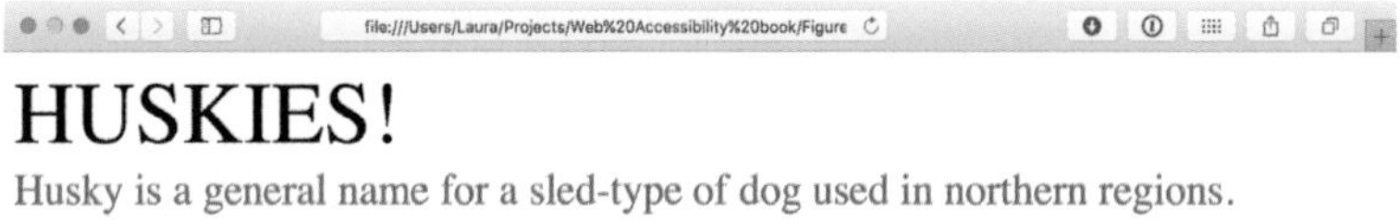

HUSKIES!

Husky is a general name for a sled-type of dog used in northern regions.

FIG 5.22: Looking good. Nice big heading, smaller subheading. The hierarchy is clear, right?

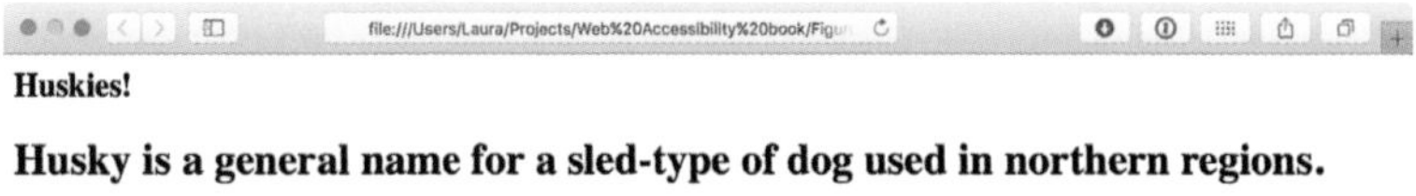

Huskies!

Husky is a general name for a sled-type of dog used in northern regions.

FIG 5.23: Without the visual style, the hierarchy of the title and subtitle are the wrong way round because that's the structure defined by the HTML.

---

h2 is big and uppercase, while the h1 is smaller and green. No wonder the h1 is being used as a subtitle.

```
<style>
  .big-title {
    display: block;
    font-size: 4em;
    text-transform: uppercase;
  }
  .green-subtitle {
    color: #01953A;
    display: block;
    font-size: 2em;
  }
</style>
<h2 class="big-title">Huskies!</h2>
<h1 class="green-subtitle">Husky is a general name
  for a sled-type of dog used in northern regions.</
  h1>
```

If you look at the same page without CSS, you can see how confusing the structure appears to screen readers and search engines (**FIG 5.23**).

Meaningful HTML

These two issues share a common root: a failure to separate structure and style. To ensure that content is meaningful to everyone—sighted users, screen readers, and search engines alike—a rigorous separation of structure and style is crucial.

HTML describes the structure and meaning of the content:

```
<h1>Huskies!</h1>
<h2>Husky is a general name for a sled-type of dog
  used in northern regions.h2>
```

CSS shapes its visual appearance:

```
<style>
  h1 {
    font-size: 4em;
    text-transform: uppercase;
  }
  h2 {
    color: #01953A;
    font-size: 2em;
  }
</style>
```

Separating structure and style has the added bonus of making HTML and CSS easier to maintain. If branding changes at a later date and we decide that all titles should be blue instead of green, we can just change the style sheet. If we were using an old WYSIWYG editor, we'd have to go through every single title and change the colors individually. That simply doesn't scale.

Fortunately, WYSIWYG editors have improved; many allow you to choose the structural element from a dropdown list (**FIG 5.24**) leading to more accurate and meaningful HTML output (**FIG 5.25**).

Even though a site's HTML is usually created by a developer or generated by a content management system, this doesn't mean we should blame the developer for badly formed HTML. With the previous examples, you can see how closely the struc-

---

FIG 5.24: The TinyMCE WYSIWYG editor in WordPress enables you to add CSS styles to the text formatting dropdown in the Visual editor view, giving writers a better idea of how their structured text will appear when published.

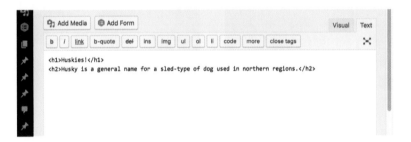

FIG 5.25: In the Text editor view, you can see that the HTML produced is meaningful and not muddied with inline CSS.

---

ture of the HTML is linked to the roles of content strategy, copywriting, and search engine optimization. Sites are likely to be much more accessible if every team member understands the impact the markup has on the content they're creating.

Alternative styles

In a world where we frequently access websites from different devices and browsers, and where pages adapt to fit a range of environments, it's not surprising that some users want to customize a site to better suit their needs.

RSS readers and browser readability extensions take the structured content of a page and display it with custom styles.

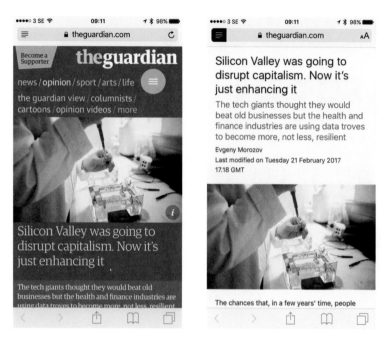

FIG 5.26: Safari's Reader view on iOS strips out the page's navigation and branding, but uses the underlying HTML to apply its own subtle (and customizable) styling.

These readers and extensions focus on making content as readable as possible by using clean typography and hiding headers, footers, and ads (**FIG 5.26**). They usually allow people to set overarching preferences for all the pages they view.

Most RSS readers and readability extensions aren't compatible with interactive pages and will strip out the visual information and behavior of interactive elements. Some extensions, such as Safari's Reader, can only be enabled on pages that contain a significant amount of text in one block.

People may rely on alternative styles if they find a site hard to read or access. This can make a site more legible or appealing, but because alternative styles only affect a site's CSS (not its structure or behavior) they can't address greater usability issues. We still need to structure our content using meaningful HTML to ensure basic accessibility.

PROGRESSIVE ENHANCEMENT AND GRACEFUL DEGRADATION

Progressive enhancement (also sometimes known as adaptive design) defines a minimal experience acceptable on all devices and browsers. Enhancements that optimize the site—for particular technologies, viewport sizes, and sometimes devices—are then layered on top of that baseline. Crucially, these enhancements don't affect access, ensuring that everyone—even those without fancy devices or the latest browsers—has a good, if basic, experience.

A simple example of progressive enhancement is adding `background-blend-mode`s to images on a site. Browsers that don't support CSS `background-blend-mode` won't parse the blend effects on the images, but the visitor's core experience isn't affected by seeing the original non-blended images instead. Visitors using browsers that *do* support CSS background-blend-mode can have an enhanced experience (**FIG 5.27**).

A more complex example of progressive enhancement is when a simple interaction has a more complex interaction layered on top. I designed a responsive accessible HTML5 video player for Ind.ie based on Dennis Lembree's accessible HTML5 video player (http://bkaprt.com/afe/05-06/). The HTML for the video player just uses the HTML video tag, which plays the source video file with the native video player provided by the user's operating system (**FIG 5.28**).

If JavaScript is enabled, a custom control panel replaces the controls of the native video player. These enhanced controls make the video player appear consistent across platforms and with the branding of the overall site, but aren't necessary to operate the video player.

A related approach is *graceful degradation*, which might be considered the flip side of the progressive enhancement coin. Graceful degradation is the idea of building for the most capable browsers, and adding fallbacks for the less capable. It's a concept borrowed from mechanical and electrical systems, designed so that when something goes wrong, the system doesn't break completely—it just operates in a limited way.

I really want to show you this photo of Oskar...

FIG 5.27: Some browsers will see the original photo (left) instead of the fancy saturated and filtered photo (right), but it's no big deal.

Internet As A Commons

Aral speaking at the European Parliament conference on "Internet as a Commons: Public Space in the Digital Age" as part of "The Big Picture" panel.

You can watch the original video on the Greens' video archive.

Internet As A Commons

Aral speaking at the European Parliament conference on "Internet as a Commons:

FIG 5.28: When you use the `video` element, the browser will use its native video player. Safari's video player is very minimalist (left). Using a custom video player meant I could add extra controls and style them to match the rest of the Ind.ie site (right).

Graceful degradation is often preferred for interaction-based sites and web apps where the primary experience of the site is built on complex behaviors rather than content. Progressive enhancement could be used to layer more complex interactions on top of simpler interactions—that is, for sites that couldn't possibly fulfill their primary purpose without any interaction at all.

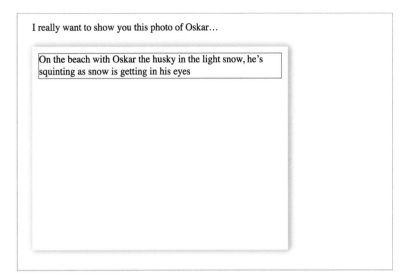

I really want to show you this photo of Oskar...

On the beach with Oskar the husky in the light snow, he's squinting as snow is getting in his eyes

FIG 5.29: The image might not be loading, but you know what you're missing because the alt text is shown.

Graceful degradation is often used in conjunction with a list of supported browsers where the site must provide the best experience. Experiences in other browsers are considered adequate if the interactive elements provide the expected response and the text is readable. A basic example of graceful degradation is when an image falls back to show only the alt text (**FIG 5.29**). The experience may not be comparable, but it's adequate.

Sites that don't provide a basic experience for all users often display an error message, telling the user to change or upgrade their browsers (**FIG 5.30**). Blocking visitors this way is generally considered lazy and bad practice. While it's reasonable to assume that an interaction-heavy site won't be able to support Internet Explorer 7, cross-browser support is a core part of building products for the modern web.

Progressive enhancement has gained favor over graceful degradation in recent years because the variety of devices and browsers has made it difficult, and unrealistic, to support only a small group of browsers. The capabilities of devices and brows-

FIG 5.30: Don't just assume that your browser is the best and everyone else wants to use it. Most visitors don't care if Clever works best in Google Chrome, and some may not know how to download another browser or have the admin privileges to do so.

ers can differ wildly from one to the next, so layering feature support and enhancements on top of a baseline experience is the easiest way to make the best site for the widest audience.

WAI-ARIA

WAI-ARIA stands for Web Accessibility Initiative—Accessible Rich Internet Applications, but it's often just referred to as "ARIA." As web standards go, ARIA is pretty new —it's only been a full-fledged web standard since March 2014. ARIA is particularly useful in conjunction with screen readers.

Complex web apps are trying to behave more like native desktop applications, and they make use of custom components or widgets to do that. These widgets allow for much richer interactions than just reading or clicking—think dragging and dropping content on the page or tracking video and audio progress using a progress bar. These complex components are usually accessible to developers in native desktop environments, but as web browsers and markup languages were originally designed with simpler, more document-based behavior in mind, browsers need extra help to understand how to make these features accessible.

WAI-ARIA allows these widgets to use different roles, states, and other properties to make it easier to describe their behavior in meaningful HTML, making them usable and recognizable by assistive technology. It also makes it possible to enhance the semantic information provided natively by HTML.

Roles

Most HTML elements have implicit roles that the browser exposes to assistive technologies as part of their default behavior. For example, an a has an implied role of link, which tells the assistive technology that this bit of HTML isn't just text but an interactive element with all the clickability and varied states that come with being a link.

WAI-ARIA's role (role=) is used as a layer on top of the existing markup language. It also helps define page structure, such as a navigation section. When an element receives focus, the screen reader understands the role this widget plays. This means the ARIA role given by the role attribute is prioritized by the browser over the implied role of the HTML element. For example, if you used a div with a role of alert, a screen reader would describe it as an alert rather than a div.

One way to understand when the role attribute should be used is when you've chosen to use a div element because the content isn't appropriately described by any other HTML element. In this case, using role might make sense to make a plain old div more accessible:

```
<div role="alert">
  <p>Your progress has been saved.</p>
</div>
```

There currently isn't an HTML element for marking up a dialog box that doesn't interrupt the user's activity, though I'm crossing my fingers that `dialog` makes it into the HTML5.2 spec. For now, we can use `role="alert"` to give the `div` alert box behavior.

Other roles include `dialog`, `status`, and `timer`. There are many roles to use with straightforward, human-readable names—you can find a full list on the W3C website (http://bkaprt.com/afe/05-07/). As when writing well-structured HTML, remember to double-check the expected meaning of the role before using it with an element.

Landmarks

Document landmarks are roles that help assistive technologies understand the role of a section and its relationship to other content on that page. Examples of document landmark roles include `navigation` and `article` (http://bkaprt.com/afe/05-08/).

While document landmarks are useful for understanding a page's structure, the idea is that you don't need these landmarks if you're already using HTML5 elements such as `nav` for navigation and `article` for an article. ARIA applied to these elements is just redundant. However, you'll want to use document landmarks for Internet Explorer, as IE has yet to provide full accessibility support for these HTML5 elements. It's worth checking Steve Faulkner's HTML5 Accessibility page (http://bkaprt.com/afe/05-09/) for information on current browser support.

States and properties

ARIA states and properties give further information about a widget to assistive technologies, thereby helping users understand how to interact with it. These states and properties are usually dynamic and can change throughout the use of the web application, most often manipulated with JavaScript. For example, the `aria-expanded` attribute might be used on a menu that expands and collapses and `aria-describedby` can tell assistive technology where to look for a description of an element.

In *Inclusive Design Patterns*, Heydon Pickering recommends using `describedby` so that assistive technology can see the connection between a password field and a password hint:

```
<label for="password">Choose a password</label>
<input type="text" id="password" aria-invalid="true"
  aria- describedby="password-hint">
<div id="password-hint">Your password must be at
  least 6 characters long</div>
```

Live regions

Live regions allow for live changes in documents to be
announced without causing people to lose focus on their
current activity. This means that those using the page can be
informed of updates without losing their place within the content. Live regions might be used when content is updated, such
as in a league table in sports, or when there's a status update in
a timeline stream.

The `aria-live` attribute is used to indicate when a widget
has a live state, and how a screen reader should introduce
changes in the widget to the user. `Aria-live="off"` means
that a region isn't currently live, and changes should not be
announced. `Aria-live="polite"` signals that the update should
be announced at the next graceful interval, such as when the
user stops typing. `Aria-live="assertive"` indicates that the
update should be announced to the user immediately:

```
<div aria-live="off">
  <p>Next update: tomorrow at 12pm CEST.</p>
</div>
<div aria-live="polite">
  <p>You have a new private message.</p>
</div>
<div aria-live="assertive">
  <p>There's a fire in the building. Please proceed
  calmly to the nearest emergency exit.</p>
</div>
```

The `assertive` property can be quite obtrusive, so it should
only be used when people need to be informed of something
immediately—such as an error or alert relevant to their current actions.

When to use ARIA (and when not to)

There are no negative side effects to using ARIA correctly, so even though there's still patchy support in some browsers, you should use it as needed. However, ARIA should never be used to replace well-structured HTML. It should be your last resort.

ARIA only interacts with the accessibility layer of a browser, so it doesn't provide the same inherent styles and behaviors that meaningful HTML provides. This also means that using ARIA won't make an unusable website more accessible. As we've discussed, an unusable site is already an inaccessible site, so using ARIA with bad copy, poorly structured HTML, and a confusing layout will result in a confusing experience for assistive technologies. If you're not sure if you need to use ARIA or not, the W3C has an easy guide for using ARIA in HTML (http://bkaprt.com/afe/05-10/).

SHOW YOUR WORK

Once our sites are built on a solid foundation of meaningful HTML, we've got the accessibility basics covered. It might seem complicated to make more complex components accessible, but accessibility standards and assistive technologies are evolving faster than ever before. Through building new components, testing them with real people, and sharing your work with other people in the web industry, you can help drive that progress.

We're fortunate that our medium, the web, enables us to iterate on the products we make. Mistakes can be fixed, alternatives can be added, products can be refined, accessibility can always be improved. Evaluation and testing helps us find problems that need fixing and create strategies for improvements.

6 EVALUATION AND TESTING

IF YOU DON'T TEST whether your accessibility efforts work, there's not much point in making the effort in the first place. Without testing, we can't tell how our site will hold up when used by real people. The success of a product will depend on whether the target audience is able to achieve their goals via their chosen technologies. These goals can therefore be used as success criteria against which the product can be tested.

MAKING A PLAN

Whenever you test or evaluate a product, you should do it against a test plan. A test plan will help you make sure you get something out of your tests, whether you're doing a formal test against standards criteria or running through tasks with a test participant. It will also make sure your tests fit in with your overall product plan. Overtesting is unlikely to be an issue, but undertesting could make you miss problems with your site.

Your testing document should contain:
- testing methods to be used, and when they'll be used in the process;
- how the testing methods will support the production team's progress toward the usability targets;
- how the test results will be documented; and
- how the test results will be fed back into the process to improve the product.

While testing is underway, keep track of any decisions you make in how you approach and conduct your tests. Writing all these decisions down will help you and others remember what worked well. When you make decisions, pay attention to how your choice of testing methods and testers could bias your results.

HEURISTICS AND ANALYSIS

Heuristic testing—the quickest way to get started—means testing against existing goals and guidelines, often conducted by the people already working on the project. It may involve prototype evaluation, code reviews, and automated tests.

Reviews of early designs and prototypes

These reviews might take the form of heuristic evaluations or cognitive walkthroughs.

Heuristic evaluations test an interface against a set of guidelines such as the WCAG, but may also take into account any common issues that aren't covered by the WCAG. If you've got your own accessibility policy, test your site against the policy's criteria. Otherwise, the WCAG 2.0 criteria cover a lot of broad use cases.

Cognitive walkthroughs test the interface against specific tasks, trying to attempt a goal in the same way a user would. These walkthroughs could also emulate a particular setup, such as someone trying to accomplish tasks using assistive technology.

Code reviews

Code reviews can be valuable early on in the process to help identify potential problems with code. Use code reviews on finished code to assess quality and consistency issues that might not be picked up during user testing (since users aren't exposed directly to the code).

Automated tests

Although automated testing alone isn't enough, automated tests *can* ensure that your code conforms to a project's standards criteria. When you're planning for automated testing, be aware that not all WCAG criteria can be programmatically verified, since many criteria focus on user experience.

Conduct automated tests near the end of production—when the code is production-ready, but there is still enough time to fix problems before the site goes live. Léonie Watson recommends including a tool like Tenon API (http://bkaprt.com/afe/06-01/) in your build process because it can catch issues long before your codebase reaches production readiness.

Twitter uses automated accessibility tests as a part of its build process as well. If a developer's code breaks the accessibility of the product, the automated test will fail and the developer is unable to deploy their work. Todd Kloots, previously a senior front-end engineer of platform at Twitter, told me he used these tests as developer education: if a developer doesn't understand why their code is failing one of the accessibility tests, Kloots had the opportunity to spread accessibility knowledge a little further.

DEVICE AND BROWSER TESTING

Device and browser testing involve testing your site across combinations of devices, operating systems, and browsers. Testing across these different conditions is a key part of accessibility testing.

It's tempting to test in your favorite browser and just hope it works in all the rest—but it probably won't. As we've seen, the web can be accessed from an incalculable array of devices, which makes it important to test on as many different devices and browsers as possible.

Choosing your testing suite

Ideally, we want our site to work with every device under the sun. However, we can realistically only test on a finite number of devices during the development stage, so it's sensible to have a list of priority devices and budget for additional devices as needed.

You need to be able to justify the devices, browsers, and assistive technologies you've chosen for testing. Did you choose them because of their market share? Their popularity among your existing users? Just because they're what you had lying around? What did your user research show?

It's impossible to test on everything, but ideally you should test with:

- desktop computers running all major operating systems (Mac OS, Windows, Linux);
- the latest version of all major desktop browsers (Opera, Safari, Firefox, Google Chrome, Internet Explorer, Microsoft Edge, Brave, or whatever's trendy nowadays) on default settings;
- mobile devices running all major operation systems (iOS, Android, Windows Phone);
- major browsers across those mobile operating systems (Safari, Firefox, Google Chrome, Opera Mini);
- assistive technologies including screen readers (JAWS, NVDU, VoiceOver, Window-Eyes, Windows Narrator, ZoomText);
- keyboard navigation; and
- a selection of prominent accessibility settings provided by the operating system and browser, such as zoom and screen magnifiers.

Virtual machines

Virtual machines such as VirtualBox and Vmware enable you to test other browsers and platforms by installing different operating systems on your computer. This can be very valuable if you're trying to test a legacy setup like Internet Explorer 7 on Windows XP, or to test a new operating system when you can't afford new hardware.

However, you should be wary of treating virtual machines as real devices. The hardware is still your computer's hardware, so it may work in a way that's less than ideal or just plain different (especially if you're running hardware with a mismatched operating system, such as testing Windows on a Mac). For example, the Windows key on the Microsoft keyboard is used for the Start menu or system-wide shortcuts. The "⌘" or Command key in the same location on the Apple keyboard is just for shortcuts, in a similar way to Microsoft's Control key.

If testers aren't aware of the mismatch between hardware and software, they'll find the product harder to use, regardless of how accessible it is.

Using a testing matrix

In a wonderful article on *A List Apart*, Anne Gibson recommended following a testing matrix with a list of outputs along the top and inputs along the side (http://bkaprt.com/afe/06-02/). The corresponding boxes should then be filled out as you test with each combination of input and output. The matrix is a great way to ensure your testing is thorough and takes many different setups into consideration (**FIG 6.1**).

Going the extra mile

If you come across issues during testing that are down to assistive technology or browser quirks, consider providing a fix for the problem rather than blaming the technology for the brokenness.

	DESKTOP COLOR SCREEN (FIREFOX)	DESKTOP COLOR SCREEN (WITH COLOR ORACLE EMULATING DEUTERANOPIA) (FIREFOX)	SMALL SMARTPHONE MAGNIFIED USING PINCH ZOOM (IPHONE 4S)	AUDIO/ SCREENREADER (MACOS VOICEOOVER)
KEYBOARD NAVIGATION (DESKTOP)	Works	Footer text needs higher contrast focus color	Not applicable	Works
MOUSE INPUT (DESKTOP)	Works	Works	Not applicable	Works
TOUCH SCREEN (IOS SAFARI)	Not applicable	Not applicable	Works, though requires a lot of horizontal scrolling to read text	Works (Tested with iOS VoiceOver)
SWITCH CONTROL (IOS)	Not applicable	Not applicable	Works	Not applicable
VOICEOVER/ DICTATION (MACOS VOICEOVER)	Works	Works	Not applicable	Works

FIG 6.1: The testing matrix ensures you don't miss a specific combination of input and output. Your testing matrix should be bigger and better!

For example, imagine that the `placeholder` attribute is being used in form input fields to give a hint on how to fill in the field. But when the user selects that input, the placeholder text vanishes to make way for the entered text. If the user can't remember the placeholder hint, they have to deselect the input so the placeholder shows again inside the input. This default behavior is less than ideal, and we might be tempted to dismiss the problem as "just how the browser works." However, there are several solutions to take that placeholder text and move it outside the input when the input is selected, giving the user a chance to fill out the form field with the hint text alongside. Brad Frost has written up a great Float Label Pattern to do exactly that (http://bkaprt.com/afe/06-03/).

Going the extra mile to solve problems like vanishing place-holders is part of embracing challenges to find creative solutions. Accessibility isn't about passing a test or ticking a box; it's about making great experiences.

VALIDATORS AND CHECKERS

There are many quick testing tools for flagging problems that might hurt the user's experience, or cause your site to render in an odd way in the browser. These validators, emulators, and checkers can be used during the design and build process to avoid common snags—whether you're writing content or code, or designing interfaces.

Validators

If you've developed websites, chances are you've used valida-tors to check that your code is valid. You paste in your URL or code, and the validator assesses it and presents you with a list of results for that page. The validator usually grades your work, telling you either that it's valid or has errors (and sometimes warnings).

However, validators have a very strict approach to reading markup. They don't understand the nuances of your code, or

FIG 6.2: Using a `meta` element with a `value` isn't valid HTML, but it is the format Twitter understands for its summary cards.

the reason you chose to use one HTML element over another. Everything is graded as wrong or right.

For this reason, validators are often better as a quick test to catch straightforward problems—code-typos, missing closing tags, and other small front-end errors—before a human who understands the context of your project makes a full assessment.

It's perfectly acceptable for your code to fail validation, as long as it fails for a good reason—like vendor-specific prefixes or browser-specific hacks.

W3C

The most well-known validator is probably W3C's markup validation tool (http://bkaprt.com/afe/06-04/), also known as the HTML validator. Among other warnings, it will inform you if you've missed a closing tag, quote mark, or required attribute, and if you've used an element where it isn't allowed, or an element or attribute that doesn't actually exist (**FIG 6.2**).

Sometimes the errors reported by the HTML validator can be difficult to understand—"literal is missing closing delimiter"—but, fortunately, a page on the validation website helps explain the errors in plain English (http://bkaprt.com/afe/06-05/). ("Literal is missing closing delimiter" usually means you've forgotten a closing quotation mark.)

FIG 6.3: WAVE results for the Ind.ie site showing "2 X Linked image missing alternative text". I better go fix that...

WebAIM's WAVE

When it comes to specialist accessibility validation tools, nothing beats WebAIM's WAVE web accessibility evaluation tool. WAVE uniquely presents the original page with icons and indicators that draw attention to accessibility errors, features, and alerts. Its focus is on helping humans evaluate web pages while also educating them about accessibility.

When you paste your URL into WAVE, it tests your markup against the WCAG guidelines. Much like the W3C HTML validator, WAVE shows you a list of errors. However, it also shows you alerts, accessibility features, structural elements, HTML5 and WAI-ARIA features, and contrast errors on your page (**FIG 6.3**). It's a nice boost to get recognition for the effort you've put into the accessibility of your site, even if it's from a bot!

If you want to test a local URL, or a site that's password-protected, you can use the WAVE toolbar for Firefox or Chrome. WebAIM is currently working on a toolbar for Microsoft Edge, too.

Color contrast checkers

Color contrast checkers are a great way to make sure the contrast of your text color is readable against the background for the majority of readers, particularly those with visual impairments and color blindness.

These checkers tend to follow a similar pattern: you enter a foreground and background color and the checker tells you if they're accessible according to the W3C color-contrast ratio guidelines. Many will show you your colors in action. Some will tell you if your color palette conforms to WCAG AA or AAA levels (we'll more look at WCAG in the next chapter). And one in particular, Color Oracle (http://bkaprt.com/afe/06-06/), will overlay the whole screen with a color filter to simulate different types of color blindness.

Readability checkers

Readability checkers test your copy for ease of reading, and usually rate the overall copy on some kind of scale, such as a school grade level. As these tests are automated, they can't replace a real person in judging whether the text is easily understood, but they can provide a rough idea of difficulty. See Resources for readability checker recommendations.

Emulating connection speeds

As mentioned earlier, technology professionals tend to enjoy much better connection speeds than average. It can be hard for us to understand how frustrating and unusable a slow site is when we've got blazing fast broadband. Connection emulation tools can throttle the speed of your internet connection to mimic mobile and other poor connection speeds. Usually tools mimic a poor connection through a proxy connection—though developer tools at the operating system level can tailor the whole native experience. See Resources for recommendations.

TESTING KEYBOARD NAVIGATION

It's not hard to test how easy your site is to browse using keyboard navigation. Most browsers just require the Tab key to move between interactive elements. Some browsers use a combination of the Tab key and a modifier key (such as Alt or Ctrl), or the Left and Right cursor keys, to move between all elements on the page. This is useful when navigating using a screen reader.

To access all elements on the page, you may have to enable a full-keyboard access setting in your operating system preferences. If you're using VoiceOver on macOS, you can use the interactive training tour available from the Accessibility panel in System Preferences to familiarize yourself with the common controls (**FIG 6.4**).

Remember, we can't make assumptions that someone using a screen reader is using keyboard navigation. Screen reader output and keyboard input should be tested both together and separately.

USABILITY TESTING

Testing with people who are likely to use your site is the best way to gauge accessibility—it's the closest you'll get to tangible scenarios.

Much like at the user research stage, it's best to conduct usability testing with people representative of your target audience and ask them to attempt to perform tasks based on your product's defined user goals. While it can be easy to test early designs and prototypes with many users, people with visual impairments, or people who rely on keyboard navigation, may find it difficult to interact with prototypes before they involve production-level code, so you'll need to factor this into your testing plan.

Try your best not to test with people who are working on the project: they will likely fail to notice the problems that might hold up other users, may not be part of the target audience at all, and are likely to have conflicting goals with other users. How

FIG 6.4: Keep in mind that screen readers can change these default keyboard commands. Léonie Watson has written a simple explanation for understanding screen reader interaction modes on her blog (http://bkaprt.com/afe/06-07/).

the intended audience really interact with a product is often different from the assumptions of a team who may know the web much better and are much more familiar with the product itself.

Finding participants

Finding participants for testing your product is similar to finding participants for user research at the start of a project. As we discussed in Chapter 3: always include people with disabilities and impairments in your testing group, and test in person to see how people use your product in context.

Choose testers who are accustomed to using the technologies they're testing with—that way you're testing the usability of your product, not their comfort with screen readers or keyboard navigation. In *Just Ask: Integrating Accessibility Throughout Design,* Shawn Henry explains:

> *Find people who are fairly experienced using products like yours. If people use assistive technologies with your product, you probably want people who are skilled with their assistive technology. Later in testing, you might want to include some novices, but early on you want people who can teach you well.*

Testing with people who use assistive technology every day will be more thorough, and will prevent you from making decisions based on potentially false assumptions about how assistive technology is used.

Be cautious when categorizing users based on their disabilities. As we explored in Chapter 2, there is such a range of ability, experience, and preferred technology setups that we can't possibly find a fully representative or comprehensive group of people covering "disability." The best we can do is work with a variety of users every time we test.

Léonie Watson reminds us to find people from our target audience for accessibility testing, not just choosing any participant because they have a disability:

> *If you're building an app for teenage girls, there's no point in asking a forty year old [sic] man to test it just because he happens to use a screen reader. In the same way his attitude and skills will be different in general, his ability to use his assistive technology will also be different from someone twenty-five years his junior.*

Decisions about the number of test participants usually comes down to expense, as participants are often paid for their time, and the team members running the tests may only have limited time. Small samples can end up with erroneous results. Larger, more expensive sample sizes might increase your confidence in the test results, though there may be diminishing returns, as the most critical usability problems are often discovered by the first few testers.

Running tests

Just as we discussed in Chapter 3, finding a facilitator to run tests can feel challenging, but it's doable. Whether your project budget is large or small, there are plenty of user research consultants and agencies who know how to help, and you'll want to work with someone who can get along well with the participants, be patient, and not lead them to complete tasks in a particular way.

It's especially difficult to be a facilitator if you're the designer or developer on a project. No matter how secure we are in our abilities, we don't like to see our work not succeed. We may be tempted to give the participants clues to make up for the failings in our prototype. If there isn't anyone on your team who can facilitate usability testing, then it's worth looking for outside help to ensure your prototype gets tested in an objective way.

You also need someone who can observe and document the test. Recording video or audio is very useful, as you can refer back to it later and don't need to worry about remembering every little detail (note that recording video or audio typically requires signed consent forms). Taking notes is also important—notes can help you remember when and where significant events occurred, and help you quickly locate these events in your recorded footage.

What to look for

Usability testing usually focuses on observing a user interacting with your product. The product could be anything from a robust prototype (you don't want anything that'll break too easily during testing!) or nearer to a finished site. Choose testing scenarios that reflect real-world use cases and involve tasks essential to the success of the product.

The benefits you'll get from a usability test depend entirely on how well you prepare beforehand, and how much attention you pay during the test. Scripting questions and tasks can help you focus on the participant and keep the session on course. It's also vital that the wording of your questions and tasks do not lead the participant towards a specific approach.

When the participant is working through the task, try to record the following:

- What are the participant's expectations? Do they already know your site? If they do, how does that impact their choices? If they are familiar with your site, perhaps follow a scenario familiar to them.
- What are the participant's first impressions? How do they approach the task? What are their initial reactions to the site?
- How does the participant flow through the task? What is the context of the scenario? How does this relate to their everyday experiences? One task at a time makes it easier to follow for both you and the participant.
- What is the participant saying and doing? Are they describing one interaction but doing something different? Are they using any particular terms and phrases to describe their interactions?
- Does the participant find any problems with the site's accessibility? Discussing any accessibility issues you come across in context is vital to understanding how the issue affects the completion of the task at hand, and how the issue may impact other areas of the site.

These are just a few suggestions that don't vary much from your garden-variety usability test. *Just Ask—Integrating Accessibility Throughout Design* also provides a practical guide to planning, conducting, and reporting usability tests with a focus on users with disabilities (http://bkaprt.com/afe/06-08/).

ONGOING TESTING

Testing doesn't end on launch day. Ongoing testing keeps accessibility at the forefront of everybody's minds when it's time to make post-launch decisions about the site. It also prevents a product from becoming less accessible over time as more and more changes are made. Test to find problems with your site, and then test your solutions. Don't just assume you'll find the right solution the first time.

Consider adding a short form to your site for ongoing testing. A simple, obvious feedback mechanism for site visitors can be a low-cost way of involving real users in testing. When you tell users that their contributions are valued, they are more likely to review and assist you in the accessibility of your product. Keep your accessibility policy in view as you assess feedback, though. All feedback should be read, replied to, and taken on board, but make sure you don't allow the feedback of a single person to divert you from needs more broadly expressed by your target audience.

Twitter has a simple feedback mechanism in their @TwitterA11y Twitter account for accessibility feedback. The @TwitterA11y account is also used to broadcast new features and potential problems (**FIG 6.5**).

Testing is really another kind of research. Testing isn't what you do at the end of a project to prove that you're brilliant at your job—it's the beginning of another iterative cycle in your project's life. Test early and often, and then test again. Regular testing will reassure you that you're heading in the right direction, or give you new targets if the accessibility falls short.

Testing can be frustrating and difficult to face as it challenges your existing assumptions about your product and its users. But it will ultimately make your product better, and you more well-informed in your future work.

Earlier in this chapter we looked briefly at how to test against standards and guidelines to generate benchmarks to aim for. But standards and guidelines aren't just nice ideas about accessibility, sometimes they're legal or regulatory requirements that need to abided by. We'll look at those next.

FIG 6.5: Have you enabled image descriptions on your Twitter settings yet? No? Go do it right now, you'll be learning to write great alt text in no time...

7
LAWS AND GUIDELINES

LET'S FACE IT, guidelines and standards are often really boring—and it can be hard to see how the principles apply in the context of your own projects. Legalese alone makes for a tough read:

> More than one way is available to locate a Web page within a set of Web pages except where the Web Page is the result of, or a step in, a process.
> —WCAG 2.0, Guideline 2.4.5

If you go over this passage carefully, you'll understand that you're being advised to give people multiple ways to reach a web page. But the text sounds fusty and formal.

There's a valid reason for that formality: these guidelines are often used as criteria for a project in the specification, or to support government-dictated standards. When any company agreement or legal requirement relies upon a text, it needs to be clear and specific. The formality of the language can make it harder to understand what you need to do to satisfy the guidelines, but W3C's Web Accessibility Initiative has plenty of additional explainers, such as the "How to Meet WCAG 2.0" quick reference (http://bkaprt.com/afe/07-01/).

THE LEGAL LANDSCAPE

People may use the legal argument as the main reason to care about accessibility, but I don't want to treat you like you're heartless. If avoiding being sued is the only reason you care about making a website available to a wide audience—particularly those with disabilities—then perhaps creating products for other people isn't for you.

That said, there have been examples in many countries (including the US and the UK) where a lack of web accessibility has been considered discriminatory against those unable to access the sites. It's important to take the legal aspects seriously.

National Federation of the Blind v. Target Corporation

In the United States, the law most relevant for accessibility is the Americans with Disabilities Act (ADA). While the act doesn't currently contain any specific references to website accessibility, a precedent was set in 2006 when three visually impaired people, alongside the National Federation of the Blind (NFB), brought a lawsuit against the American retailer Target.

The court ruled that commercial websites such as Target. com are required to be accessible under the ADA and state laws. Target never admitted that its website was inaccessible, but was required to comply with NFB certification. Target also had to pay the NFB a total of $170,000 for certification over three years, give its web developers at least one day of accessibility training, and pay damages to the class-action claimants.

UK law and RNIB v. Bmibaby Limited

In the UK, the relevant accessibility law is the Equality Act. Section 20 of the Equality Act, "Duty to make adjustments," refers specifically to the accessibility of information:

Where the first [a disabled person at a substantial disadvantage in comparison to someone who is not disabled] or third [where a disabled person would, but for the provision of an auxiliary aid, be put at a substantial disadvantage to someone who is not disabled] requirement relates to the provision of information, the steps which it is reasonable for A [a person who has a duty to provide information] to have to take include steps for ensuring that in the circumstances concerned the information is provided in an accessible format.

That's a very long-winded way of saying that information (including websites) should be provided in an accessible format so that people with disabilities aren't at a substantial disadvantage compared to those without disabilities.

In 2012, the Royal National Institute of Blind People (RNIB) threatened the UK airline Bmibaby Limited with legal action for "failing to ensure web access for blind and partially sighted customers." After attempting to give Bmibaby advice and guidance, the RNIB started legal proceedings (though the case was never brought to court). Four months later, the following statement appeared on the RNIB website:

RNIB is pleased BMI baby [sic] has finally listened to their blind customers, and RNIB, and made changes to its website which now enable blind people to book flights. Prior to the changes blind people visiting the website weren't even able to select their flight dates as they were only able to do so by using a mouse. Blind people are unable to use a computer mouse because they're not able to see the arrow on screen which would be used to select holidays dates.

There are a few other issues which BMI baby need to fix, such as making it possible for a blind person to pre-book their seat. Currently this part of the website isn't accessible to blind people. BMI baby and RNIB are looking into these issues and giving consideration as to whether it is now possible to settle the legal proceedings.

—Sam Fothergill, RNIB Senior Legal Policy Officer, 27th April 2012

When I speak to accessibility professionals, many tell me of cases with equally high-profile companies quietly settling out of court. Many companies don't want the bad publicity and exposure of an inaccessible website. They would rather pay money to the claimants and improve their sites out of the public eye.

CURRENT LEGISLATION AND AGREEMENTS

Many countries have their own standards and laws covering the web and accessibility. Often web accessibility is folded into other access and disability discrimination laws. In the US, the law you're most likely to come across is Section 508 (the US standard). In Europe, we have the European Accessibility Act.

Section 508

Section 508 is an amendment made in 1998 to the US Rehabilitation Act of 1973. It's a regulation that requires that all US federal employees with disabilities have the same access to information as employees without disabilities. It also requires that electronic and information technology from US federal agencies is accessible to people with disabilities. Section 508 doesn't require compliance from non-government sites unless they receive federal funds or are under contract with a federal agency.

Section 508's "refresh" was published in the Federal Register in January 2017 after a long period of consultation and changes going back to 2008. Matt Feldman has covered the update in detail on the Paciello Group website (http://bkaprt. com/afe/07-02/)

The refreshed standards give instructions for specific types and uses of technology, including the notable recommendation that sites should adhere to Level A and Level AA of the WCAG 2.0 guidelines—exactly what Dale Cruse, senior digital accessibility specialist at JPMorgan Chase, suggests doing:

Those are good guidelines, but they only apply to the United States of America. I worked at a global organization focused on learning solutions for all people. Instead of Section 508, I turned our attention to WCAG 2.0 Level AA standards. That way, as an organization, we could talk about the same guidelines and the same goals. We had a common understanding of what we were trying to achieve together.

We'll have a look at the WCAG later in this chapter.

The European Accessibility Act

The European Union has a similar draft regulation to Section 508 in its European Accessibility Act (http://bkaprt.com/afe/07-03/). It's a directive designed to create a legislative framework for accessibility in line with Article 9 of the United Nation's Convention on the Rights of Persons with Disabilities (CRPD). The Convention has two underlying principles that particularly apply to web accessibility: recognizing the importance of full and effective participation and inclusion in society, and the accessibility of information and communication technology. The European Accessibility Act doesn't just cover websites and computers, but also the digital aspects of other public systems, such as ATMs and ticketing machines.

GUIDELINES

The legal stuff can seem pretty scary, but as I mentioned earlier, standards and guidelines help us generate benchmark for our work. Guidelines like the Web Content Accessibility Guidelines (WCAG) act as valuable checks at various stages of a website's creation and maintenance, giving us structure when we're deciding how to develop a site.

WCAG

WCAG 2.0 is the current version of the Web Content Accessibility Guidelines from the W3C. Developed by the Web Accessibility Initiative (WAI), WCAG 2.0 distinctly differs from WCAG 1.0 in the sense that the W3C shifted its approach away from specific technologies. In WCAG 1.0, the checkpoints within each guideline frequently refer to particular technologies (links, image maps, form controls):

> *9.5 Provide keyboard shortcuts to important links (including those in client-side image maps), form controls, and groups of form controls.*

That's still good advice, but it's very specific. The WCAG 2.0 guidelines are broader and more technology-independent so that they can be easily applied to unanticipated, new web technologies. Every guideline is structured as an overarching principle, containing corresponding guidelines that each have success criteria. In WCAG 2.0, the closest we get to that same guideline is:

> *2.1.1 Keyboard: All functionality of the content is operable through a keyboard interface without requiring specific timings for individual keystrokes, except where the underlying function requires input that depends on the path of the user's movement and not just the endpoints.*

Even this brief example makes clear that the success criteria apply to "all functionality of the content" (which I would call interaction)—not just links, image maps, and form controls.

Principles

The WCAG 2.0 principles are focused around a human-centered approach to web design, and handily spell out the acronym POUR (Perceivable, Operable, Understandable, Robust):

- **Principle 1:** Perceivable—information and user interface components must be presentable to users in ways they can perceive.
- **Principle 2:** Operable—user interface components and navigation must be operable.
- **Principle 3:** Understandable—information and the operation of user interface must be understandable.
- **Principle 4:** Robust—content must be robust enough that it can be interpreted reliably by a wide variety of user agents, including assistive technologies.

Without looking at the guidelines underneath these principles, it may seem that "perceivable" and "understandable" are the same thing, but they're not. "Perceivable" is about being able to access the content in the first place. "Understandable" is about then being able to understand the content so that you can interact with it.

It's not going too far to say that I love the WCAG 2.0 principles. They're not just overarching themes for each group of guidelines, but also general principles that can be understood by everybody in an organization. Their entire focus is on making a site that's easy to use, regardless of the technology you're using. It's well worth bookmarking the principles so you can easily refer to them while you're creating a site. They're free, so you haven't got an excuse not to.

Levels

WCAG has multiple levels of conformance. Each success criteria in the WCAG 2.0 guideline is designed to be testable. To conform to WCAG 2.0, you need to meet these criteria. (http://bkaprt.com/afe/07-01/) Each criteria has a level:

- Level A: the lowest (minimum) level of conformance
- Level AA: the middle level of conformance, satisfying both Level A and Level AA criteria
- Level AAA: the highest level of conformance, satisfying Level A, Level AA, and Level AAA criteria

Most organizations interested in accessibility aim for Level AA. The standards and laws in some countries require that government sites conform to Level AA. Agencies proposing site redesigns to big companies will often find Level AA is required in the specification, as it minimizes the chance of legal action against the company.

Organizations that specialize in accessibility and inclusion aim toward Level AAA. It's the hardest level to achieve, and may require a lot of additional time and expense to meet criteria such as:

> *1.2.6 Sign Language (Prerecorded): Sign language interpretation is provided for all prerecorded audio content in synchronized media. (Level AAA)*
>
> *1.2.7 Extended Audio Description (Prerecorded): Where pauses in foreground audio are insufficient to allow audio descriptions to convey the sense of the video, extended audio description is provided for all prerecorded video content in synchronized media. (Level AAA)*

Sign language and audio descriptions are very worthwhile but require specialist skills, software, and a lot of time—depending on the amount of audio on your site. Many organizations can't afford these costs and are therefore unable to comply with Level AAA.

If you're new to accessibility, especially if you're working with an existing site, start with Level A. You'll probably find that as you begin thinking about people using your site in a new way, and implementing the more straightforward guidelines, you'll end up complying with the stricter levels anyway. For example, you may intend to make your text accessible following the guideline on distinguishable content:

> *Guideline 1.4 Distinguishable: Make it easier for users to see and hear content including separating foreground from background.*

In doing so, you make your text a dark color on a light background. When checking the color contrast ratio, you discover that it happens to conform to Level AA:

1.4.3 Contrast (Minimum): The visual presentation of text and images of text has a contrast ratio of at least 4.5:1 (Level AA)

ATAG

If you're working on producing content management systems, or a web app that allows the user to write content and upload images, the W3C has specialized guidelines for what it considers "authoring tools"—the Authoring Tool Accessibility Guidelines (ATAG).

It's unlikely that the owners of social networks and other authoring tools will be held to account for the accessibility of the content their users produce. But it's just good practice to enable your users to make their content accessible. What's the point in making your tool accessible if the content created with it isn't?

ATAG has two parts:

- ensuring the authoring element of site is accessible
- ensuring the authoring element helps users produce accessible content

Much like WCAG 2.0, ATAG 2.0 is arranged with overarching principles, specific guidelines, and success criteria with A, AA, and AAA levels.

Beyond guidelines

Remember, you can stick to laws, standards, and guidelines without feeling restricted by them. Moreover, we can use these standards and guidelines to help us plan better sites and as a benchmark against which to evaluate our work. If you care about a site's accessibility, you're unlikely to be on the wrong side of the law.

It can be easy to treat guidelines as checklists—criteria to simply tick off, convinced of our compliance. That might satisfy a court, but it ignores the principles underlying the guidelines.

The point of web accessibility is to create flexible and generous sites that benefit people using the web. When we focus on checklists, we're only "doing" accessibility so we don't get told off by the authorities, not because we care about great experiences for fellow users of the web. And if we don't care about great experiences, and are only doing the bare minimum to adhere to the guidelines, we're not going to create good websites.

KEEPING UP

The wonder of technology is that it's constantly evolving and at breathtaking speed. The stress of technology is that we feel compelled to keep up.

If you work in technology, you're probably painfully aware of how many new technologies and best practices you need to stay on top of to do your job well. New devices, operating systems, browsers, and assistive technologies come out every day, and they all affect accessibility work.

When you're trying to keep up with the accessibility landscape, look out for new assistive technologies, changes to accessibility support in browsers and operating systems, and breakthroughs in front-end technologies. Keep your ears out and your eyes open so you can retest sites on updated versions of your testing suite when necessary. The blogs listed in the Resources section will also help you stay up to date.

In contrast to the dizzying pace of technological change, accessibility best practices tend to evolve much less frequently. Accessibility is not so much about technological developments as it is about finding lots of little ways to improve on current technology and experiences.

Do the right thing

Doing accessibility well is about merging your knowledge of accessibility with your project's context to create a balance that serves the people who use your site.

Your types of content and interactions will dictate one set of constraints. Your visitors' needs and goals will dictate another. In broad terms, the whole of web design as a practice is finding the equilibrium between these constraints.

Don't let accessibility overwhelm you. Everything I've written in this book really comes down to these tips:

- Being considerate is the first steps to an accessible site. Accessibility is easy to consider once you start caring about it. Once you start thinking about accessibility at every point of planning, you'll apply it to the content, interactions, aesthetics, and code.
- The key to universality in web design lies in being flexible. We need to embrace the natural flexibility of the web. It's not about relinquishing all control, or making things generic, or dumbing them down. Research and testing will help us understand where we need to be flexible—and where we need constraints—to make a site accessible to as many people as possible. We need to use our knowledge to understand where to set the boundaries.
- Use guidelines as just that: guidelines. Once you've absorbed the requirements for broad web accessibility, you can use policies and guidelines to make sure you don't forget important details during production. But strict adherence to rules doesn't ensure good accessibility—you need to understand the audience and balance their needs, rather than just ticking boxes.

As we wrap up our time together, I have a final request for you: talk about accessibility more! If you do, others will too. My one wish for the web is that people consider accessibility in the same way they think about web performance. The performance implications of a new tool or technique are always mentioned in blog posts and articles. Wouldn't it be great if the same were true for accessibility?

We need to work together to make and keep the web open, affordable, and available to all. Accessibility is our way to ensure that *nobody* gets shut out.

RESOURCES

Accessibility

Check these blogs and sites regularly to benefit from the know-how of the accessibility experts.

- The A11y Project. Accessibility patterns, checklists, and resources for web developers (http://bkaprt.com/afe/08-01/).
- Heydonworks. Heydon Pickering's blog is packed with useful code examples and thoughtful blog posts about accessibility and design (http://bkaprt.com/afe/08-02/).
- The Paciello Group. Many of the accessibility experts you'll hear about work for The Paciello Group. Needless to say, their blog is usually the first place to read about accessibility news (http://bkaprt.com/afe/08-03/).
- Tink.uk. Léonie Watson is prolific and writes the most easy-to-understand explanations about accessibility you'll find on the web (http://bkaprt.com/afe/08-04/).
- Axess Lab. A small agency focused on building accessible products and spreading awareness of accessibility (http://bkaprt.com/afe/08-05/).
- Simply Accessible. An agency full of accessibility experts who write regularly about their work (http://bkaprt.com/afe/08-06/).
- Web Axe. Accessibility blog and podcast run by Dennis Lembree featuring accessibility news and tips (http://bkaprt.com/afe/08-07/).

Accessible code patterns

- *Inclusive Design Patterns*, Heydon Pickering. An informative book packed with accessible front-end design patterns for web interfaces (http://bkaprt.com/afe/08-08/).
- "Float Label Pattern," Brad Frost. A pattern for creating floating label placeholders, including a look at pros, cons and extra resources (http://bkaprt.com/afe/06-03/).

- "Maintaining Accessibility in a Responsive World," Scott Jehl. Accessibility considerations and patterns that Filament Group use in their work (http://bkaprt.com/afe/08-09/).

Animation

- "Designing Safer Web Animation For Motion Sensitivity," Val Head. This article covers the whys and hows of designing for vestibular disorders and seizures (http://bkaprt.com/afe/02-04/).

ARIA

- "Accessible Rich Internet Applications (WAI-ARIA) 1.0." The W3C Candidate Recommendation for ARIA (http://bkaprt.com/afe/08-10/).
- "Using ARIA." The W3C's easy guide for using ARIA in HTML (http://bkaprt.com/afe/05-10/).

Assistive technology

- "All Technology Is Assistive: Six Design Rules on 'Disability'," Sara Hendren. (http://bkaprt.com/afe/04-01/).
- "Use Switch Control to navigate your iPhone, iPad, or iPod touch." Apple's support page on how to use Switch Control (http://bkaprt.com/afe/08-11/).
- "macOS Sierra: Use Dwell Control." Apple's support page on how to use Dwell Control (http://bkaprt.com/afe/08-12/).
- Natural Reader, the text-to-speech tool (http://bkaprt.com/afe/02-03/).
- "Understanding screen reader interaction modes," Léonie Watson. Goes over screen reader virtual/browse, forms/focus, and applications modes (http://bkaprt.com/afe/06-07/).
- "Using Narrator dev mode," Léonie Watson. A brief explanation about how to use Windows screen reader developer mode (http://bkaprt.com/afe/01-02/).
- "How to Make Your Website Accessible to People Who Use a Screen Magnifier," Frederik Creemers. Gives some tips for catering to screen magnifiers (http://bkaprt.com/afe/08-13/).

- "What I've learned about motor impairment," James Williamson. James explains how to improve usability for people with motor impairments, based on his own experiences (http://bkaprt.com/afe/08-14/).

Color and design

- *Color Accessibility Workflows*, Geri Coady. Goes in-depth on designing for color accessibility, with loads of tools and workflow recommendations (http://bkaprt.com/afe/08-15/).
- Color Contrast Analyser. The Paciello Group's Windows and Mac app helps you determine the legibility of text by checking the contrast between your text color and background color against WCAG2 criteria (http://bkaprt.com/afe/08-16/).
- Colour Contrast Check. Jonathan Snook's checker is similar to The Paciello Group's tool, but is web-based (http://bkaprt.com/afe/08-17/).
- Contrast Ratio. Lea Verou's color contrast tool that can also calculate the accessibility of transparent colors (http://bkaprt.com/afe/08-18/).
- Color Oracle. Desktop tool for Mac OS, Windows, and Linux that simulates deuteranopia, protanopia, and tritanopia color blindness by overlaying the whole screen with a color filter (http://bkaprt.com/afe/06-06/).

CSS

- "5 Powerful Tips And Tricks For Print Style Sheets," Dudley Storey (http://bkaprt.com/afe/04-09/).
- "CSS Tricks Finally Gets A Print Stylesheet," Chris Coyier (http://bkaprt.com/afe/04-10/).

HTML

- "Accessibility APIs: A Key to Web Accessibility," Léonie Watson and Chaals McCathie Nevile. An introduction to the history and current state of how browsers provide accessibility and how we can write accessible HTML (http://bkaprt.com/afe/08-19/).

- HTML5 Accessibility. Reference tables comparing the accessibility implementation of HTML5 elements (http://bkaprt.com/afe/08-20/).
- HTML5 Doctor. Reference site looking at the purpose and benefit of HTML5 elements (http://bkaprt.com/afe/08-21/).
- *HTML5 for Web Designers*, Jeremy Keith and Rachel Andrew. An introduction to all the HTML5 you need to know (http://bkaprt.com/afe/08-22/).
- "HTML element reference." Mozilla Developer Network's handy reference of HTML elements and their purposes and benefits (http://bkaprt.com/afe/08-23/).
- "The Truth About Multiple H1 Tags in the HTML5 Era," Kezz Bracey. A thorough write-up on document outlines and multiple h1s (http://bkaprt.com/afe/08-24/).
- "Time to revisit accesskey?" Léonie Watson reviews the accessibility benefits and negatives of the accesskey attribute (http://bkaprt.com/afe/05-03/).
- "Links are not buttons. Neither are DIVs and SPANs," Karl Groves. Covers the differences between links and buttons and how to mark them up accessibly (http://bkaprt.com/afe/08-25/).

Guidelines

- "Web Content Accessibility Guidelines (WCAG) 2.0." The W3C's Recommendation (http://bkaprt.com/afe/08-26/).
- "How to Meet WCAG 2.0." Customizable, quick reference to Web Content Accessibility Guidelines 2.0 requirements (success criteria) and techniques (http://bkaprt.com/afe/07-01/).
- "Ethical Design Manifesto." How accessibility fits into wider ethical design (http://bkaprt.com/afe/08-27/).
- "Inclusive Design Principles." The Paciello Group's broad guidelines to inclusive design (http://bkaprt.com/afe/08-28/).

Internationalization

- "Styling vertical Chinese, Japanese, Korean and Mongolian text," (http://bkaprt.com/afe/08-29/).
- "Creating HTML Pages in Arabic, Hebrew and Other Right-to-left Scripts (tutorial)," (http://bkaprt.com/afe/08-30/).

Planning and research

- *Just Enough Research*, Erika Hall. Focuses on the value of research and how to do it effectively for your web projects (http://bkaprt.com/afe/03-01/).

Performance

- "Accessibility and Performance," Marcy Sutton. A look at how to improve performance for people using assistive technology (http://bkaprt.com/afe/08-31/).
- Network Link Conditioner. An Apple developer tool that enables you to simulate different network connection speeds with a variety of preset connections, including 3G, Edge, and the amusingly named "Very Bad Network" (http://bkaprt. com/afe/08-32/, requires Apple Developer account).
- Charles. A paid desktop app for OS X, Windows, and Linux that creates a proxy connection for the internet and throttles it using custom settings (http://bkaprt.com/afe/08-33/).

Typography

- Butterick's Practical Typography. Matthew Butterick's guide to typography (http://bkaprt.com/afe/08-34/).
- Heinemann Typeface. By Heinemann Publishing and available on MyFonts (http://bkaprt.com/afe/08-35/).
- *On Web Typography*, Jason Santa Maria. Gives insight into how to make your content usable and beautiful (http:// bkaprt.com/afe/04-04/).

- "The Elements of Typographic Style Applied to the Web," Richard Rutter. Resource applying the principles from Robert Bringhurst's *The Elements of Typographic Style* to the web (http://bkaprt.com/afe/08-36/).
- "Using UI System Fonts In Web Design: A Quick Practical Guide," Marcin Wichary. Guide on how to implement system UI fonts reliably cross-browser (http://bkaprt.com/afe/08-37/).
- "What is a Web Safe Font?" CoffeeCup Software's concise article on web-safe fonts (http://bkaprt.com/afe/08-38/).

Subtitles and captions

- Caption and Subtitle Format Converter. 3PlayMedia's web-based tool that can convert a Web Subtitle Resource Track (.srt) to WebVTT (.vtt) (http://bkaprt.com/afe/08-39/).
- Jubler Subtitle Editor. A desktop captions and subtitle editor for OS X, Windows, and Linux that requires Java (http://bkaprt.com/afe/08-40/).
- Subtitle Horse: Online Subtitle/Captions Editor. A web-based captions editor that requires Flash (http://bkaprt.com/afe/08-41/).

SVG

- *Practical SVG,* Chris Coyier. Makes SVG easy to understand with plenty of tips and tricks (http://bkaprt.com/afe/04-07/).
- "Tips for Creating Accessible SVG," Léonie Watson. How to make your SVG graphics more accessible (http://bkaprt.com/afe/08-42/).

Usability

- *A Web For Everyone: Designing Accessible User Experiences,* Sarah Horton and Whitney Quesenbery. A look at how universal design principles can be applied during the design and development process (http://bkaprt.com/afe/02-43/).
- "How do blind people interpret emoji's?" The BBC's Ouch: Disability Talk podcast team discuss whether emojis are

accessible and how their use can be confusing (http://bkaprt.com/afe/08-44/).

- "Disabled Buttons Suck," Hampus Sethfors. Examples of the usability issues around the disabled button state (http://bkaprt.com/afe/08-45/).
- *Design For Real Life*, Sara Wachter-Boettcher and Eric Meyer. How to design products more compassionately, understanding that people use your products in unexpected ways and at unexpected times (http://bkaprt.com/afe/02-09/).
- *Just Ask: Integrating Accessibility Throughout Design* by Shawn Henry. Goes through the whole design process with an eye to accessibility (http://bkaprt.com/afe/08-46/).
- "'Skip Navigation' Links." WebAIM's thorough guide to skip links including browser quirks and alternative options (http://bkaprt.com/afe/08-47/).
- "Sounding out the web: accessibility for deaf and hard of hearing people [Part 1]." David Swallow talks to Ruth Mac-Mullen about her experience of being deaf and how it affects her use of the web (http://bkaprt.com/afe/08-48/).
- "Accessibility with Dale Cruse." Jen Simmons talks to Dale Cruse on The Web Ahead podcast (http://bkaprt.com/afe/01-01/).
- "What Non-Disabled People Get Wrong About Accessibility." Liam explains common misconceptions about accessibility (http://bkaprt.com/afe/08-49/).
- "Accessibility According To Actual People with Disabilities." Hampus Sethfors categories and summarises the tweets in response to Safia Abdalla's question: "if you have a disability, what's the hardest thing about browsing the web?" (http://bkaprt.com/afe/05-50/)

Validators and inspectors

- Web Developer Browser Extension. Before browser web inspectors were any good, there was Chris Pederick's Web Developer Extension. It still has loads of handy tools (http://bkaprt.com/afe/08-51/).
- HTML5 Outliner. A web tool and bookmarklet for checking your HTML5 outlines (http://bkaprt.com/afe/08-52/).

Video

- Universal Video Player. A responsive, accessible HTML5 video player for Ind.ie based on Dennis Lembree's accessible HTML5 video player (http://bkaprt.com/afe/05-06/).

Writing and readability

- Center for Plain Language. Guidance for writing in plain language for government agencies and businesses (http://bkaprt.com/afe/08-53/).
- "18F Content Guide." The US government's digital service guide on how to plan, write, and manage content (http://bkaprt.com/afe/08-54/).
- "Conscious Style Guide." A collection of guides and articles focusing on how to use inclusive language (http://bkaprt.com/afe/08-55/).
- "Writing for GOV.UK: How to write well for your audience, including specialists." The UK's Government Digital Service's guide has a lot of advice on how to write for an audience as broad as an entire country, as well as specialists (http://bkaprt.com/afe/08-56/).
- Juicy Studio Readability Test. Gez Lemon has created a very useful readability test that examines web pages for their readability according to the Gunning Fog Index, Flesch Reading Ease, and Flesch-Kincaid grade-level algorithms (http://bkaprt.com/afe/08-57/).
- Hemingway App. A writing tool that helps you evaluate your copy for readability using scores for US school grades 0-18 (http://bkaprt.com/afe/08-58/).

ACKNOWLEDGEMENTS

I wrote a book! And this book certainly wouldn't have happened without the effort of a huge number of people. To start, I'm endlessly grateful to Katel LeDû, Jason Santa Maria, and Jeffrey Zeldman. I wouldn't have been able to write a book if they hadn't put their confidence in me in the first place. Across an ocean and a continent, Katel has kept this project on course, stuck with me, and been there for all my daft questions. I am indebted to her and the amazing team she assembled to make this book happen. A Book Apart is really something special.

Many thanks to the incredible editors—Erin Kissane, Caren Litherland, and Lisa Maria Martin—without whom my text on accessibility would not have been an accessible read. They taught me about writing, gave my words shape, turned the book upside down, shook the rough bits out, and put it all back together again—all while being both inspiring and generous.

Thanks to Jason Santa Maria (again) for the beautiful design, Tina Lee for keeping things running smoothly, and everyone else at A Book Apart whose hard work makes their library so indispensable.

Through a decade of working with the web, I've learned so much from accessibility experts and advocates. They deserve the most thanks for the ideas in this book. Two of these wonderful people are Léonie Watson and Sarah Horton—not only have they been leaders in inclusive design, they have also always been kind and supportive of my work. Thanks also to those who gave me their time and knowledge along the way, especially: Chris Mills, Henny Swan, Jeremy Keith, Anna Debenham, Stephane Deschamps, Todd Kloots, Marcy Sutton, Jonathan Snook, Kimberley Tew, Jared Smith, Lea Verou, Nathaniel Vaughn Kelso, Yvonne Aburrow, Simon Cox, Anne Gibson, Alice Boxhall, Bruce Lawson, Heydon Pickering, and Dale Cruse.

Oskar should be thanked even though he won't read this—he's my shadow, walking companion, and the most beautiful (if reluctant) model for the photos in this book. I will pay him gratitude in carrots.

All my love and thanks to my family—the whole lot of you. Your unending excitement for me has really kept me going. I know how lucky I am to have you all, and that you'll read this book even though you don't make websites! Kisses and hugs to Daddy, E, Nini, and Bun—I love you so much. Thanks also to my friends who put up with my rattling on about this book for such a long time.

Thank you to Aral, for always pushing me to do more important and meaningful things. Thank you for being my biggest champion, helping me know my worth, and never complaining when I took time away from our work to write. I am incredibly lucky to have you as my partner in both work and love.

Finally, Sam. Thank you for being the best brother, and for helping me so much with this book. It's funny how a person can inspire your work so much, yet you don't even realize it until you write a book about it. Thank you for your wisdom and advice, and for being the nicest person on the planet.

REFERENCES

Shortened URLs are numbered sequentially; the related long URLs are listed below for reference.

Chapter 1

01-01   http://thewebahead.net/64

01-02   http://tink.uk/using-narrator-dev-mode/

01-03   https://www.flickr.com/photos/karola/4017466586/

Chapter 2

02-01   https://pixabay.com/en/kingfisher-bird-aviary-color-nature-863495/

02-02   https://www.bdadyslexia.org.uk

02-03   http://www.naturalreaders.com/index.html

02-04   https://alistapart.com/article/designing-safer-web-animation-for-motion-sensitivity

02-05   https://www.w3.org/TR/UNDERSTANDING-WCAG20/seizure-does-not-violate.html

02-06   http://www.gartner.com/newsroom/id/3270418

02-07   http://www.prnewswire.com/news-releases/joint-study-from-aol-and-bbdo-turns-traditional-view-of-mobile-space-on-its-head-172448781.html

02-08   https://www.iab.com/news/nearly-two-thirds-of-mobile-phone-video-usage-happens-at-home-providing-cross-media-opportunities-for-marketers-according-to-iab-mobile-study/

02-09   https://abookapart.com/products/design-for-real-life

Chatper 3

03-01   https://abookapart.com/products/just-enough-research

03-02   http://www.uiaccess.com/JustAsk/

03-03   http://www.postoffice.co.uk/accessibility#Overview

Chapter 4

04-01   https://backchannel.com/all-technology-is-assistive-ac9f7183c8cd

04-02   https://www.flickr.com/photos/ansik/3318806932/

04-03   http://techcrunch.com/2014/03/12/googles-search-results-ditch-the-underlined-links-increase-the-font-size-more-in-new-experiment/

04-04   https://abookapart.com/products/on-web-typography

04-05   http://www.book.webtypography.net

04-06   https://symbolset.com

04-07   https://abookapart.com/products/practical-svg

04-08   https://www.pineapplejazz.com/socialcooling/

04-09   https://www.smashingmagazine.com/2013/03/tips-and-tricks-for-print-style-sheets/

04-10   https://css-tricks.com/css-tricks-finally-gets-a-print-stylesheet/

04-11   https://ind.ie/blog/accessible-video-player/

Chapter 5

05-01   http://chrispederick.com/work/web-developer/

05-02   https://support.google.com/webmasters/answer/35769

05-03   http://tink.uk/time-to-revisit-accesskey/

05-04   https://www.flickr.com/photos/lascribe/74281180/in/photolist-6qgJ9R-7u1pG-7JWbxE-6gdn5f-jCpokm-7yHd1-qoEex-qoEfa-NY1gf-b6ZcG-FKRiC-5tzzp-8DGuxT-a65B3-x8Anm-fB8qzv-v41k8-5EeCEL-MfHSP-9WuFb9-6nFod1-P3MQeN-BFXZL-4FYPd

05-05   http://laurakalbag.com/skip-links/#li-comment-137909

05-06   https://source.ind.ie/project/video-player

05-07   https://www.w3.org/TR/wai-aria-1.1/#roles_categorization

05-08   https://www.w3.org/TR/wai-aria/roles#landmark_roles

05-09   http://stevefaulkner.github.io/HTML5accessibility/

05-10   https://www.w3.org/TR/aria-in-html/

Chapter 6

06-01   http://www.adlib-recruitment.co.uk/blog/is-your-web-presence-accessible-to-everyone/

06-01   http://alistapart.com/article/reframing-accessibility-for-the-web

06-02   http://bradfrost.com/blog/post/float-label-pattern/

06-03   http://validator.w3.org/

06-04   http://validator.w3.org/docs/errors.html

06-05   http://www.cololoracle.org/

06-06   http://tink.uk/understanding-screen-reader-interaction-modes/

06-07   http://www.uiaccess.com/accessucd/ut.html

Chapter 7

07-01 https://www.w3.org/WAI/WCAG20/quickref/

07-02 https://www.paciellogroup.com/blog/2017/01/section-508-refresh-part-1/

07-03 http://ec.europa.eu/social/main.jsp?catId=1202

Resources

08-01 http://a11yproject.com

08-02 http://www.heydonworks.com

08-03 https://www.paciellogroup.com/blog/

08-04 https://tink.uk/

08-05 https://axesslab.com/articles/

08-06 http://simplyaccessible.com/archives/

08-07 http://www.webaxe.org

08-08 https://www.smashingmagazine.com/inclusive-design-patterns/

08-09 https://www.filamentgroup.com/lab/accessible-responsive.html

08-10 https://www.w3.org/TR/wai-aria/

08-11 https://support.apple.com/en-us/HT201370

08-12 https://support.apple.com/kb/PH25153

08-13 https://dev.to/_bigblind/how-to-make-your-website-accessible-to-people-who-use-a-screen-magnifier

08-14 http://simpleprimate.com/blog/motor

08-15 https://abookapart.com/products/color-accessibility-workflows

08-16 http://www.paciellogroup.com/resources/contrastanalyser/

08-17 http://www.snook.ca/technical/colour_contrast/colour.html

08-18 https://leaverou.github.io/contrast-ratio/

08-19 https://www.smashingmagazine.com/2015/03/web-accessibility-with-accessibility-api/

08-20 http://html5accessibility.com

08-21 http://html5doctor.com

08-22 https://abookapart.com/products/html5-for-web-designers

08-23 https://developer.mozilla.org/en-US/docs/Web/HTML/Element

08-24 http://webdesign.tutsplus.com/articles/the-truth-about-multiple-h1-tags-in-the-html5-era--webdesign-16824

08-25 http://www.karlgroves.com/2013/05/14/links-are-not-buttons-neither-are-divs-and-spans/

08-26 https://www.w3.org/TR/WCAG20/

08-27 https://ind.ie/ethical-design

08-28 http://inclusivedesignprinciples.org

08-29 https://www.w3.org/International/articles/vertical-text/

08-30 https://www.w3.org/International/tutorials/bidi-xhtml/

08-31 https://marcysutton.com/accessibility-and-performance/

08-32 https://developer.apple.com/download/more/?q=Network%20Link%20Conditioner

08-33 http://www.charlesproxy.com

08-34 http://practicaltypography.com

08-35 https://www.myfonts.com/fonts/fw-heinemann/heinemann/

08-36 http://webtypography.net/toc/

08-37 https://www.smashingmagazine.com/2015/11/using-system-ui-fonts-practical-guide/

08-38 http://www.coffeecup.com/help/articles/what-is-a-web-safe-font/

08-39 http://www.3playmedia.com/services-features/tools/captions-format-converter/

08-40 http://www.jubler.org

08-41 http://www.subtitle-horse.com

08-42 https://www.sitepoint.com/tips-accessible-svg/

08-43 http://rosenfeldmedia.com/books/a-web-for-everyone/

08-44 http://www.bbc.co.uk/programmes/p048v3kl

08-45 https://axesslab.com/disabled-buttons-suck/

08-46 http://www.uiaccess.com/accessucd/

08-47 http://webaim.org/techniques/skipnav/

08-48 https://www.paciellogroup.com/blog/2017/02/sounding-out-the-web-accessibility-for-deaf-and-hard-of-hearing-people-part-1/

08-49 https://yetanotherlefty.wordpress.com/2017/05/01/what-non-disabled-people-get-wrong-about-accessibility

08-50 https://axesslab.com/accessibility-according-to-pwd/

08-51 http://chrispederick.com/work/web-developer/

08-52 https://hoyois.github.io/html5outliner/

08-53 http://centerforplainlanguage.org

08-54 https://content-guide.18f.gov/index.html

08-55 http://consciousstyleguide.com

08-56 https://www.gov.uk/guidance/content-design/writing-for-gov-uk

08-57 http://juicystudio.com/services/readability.php

08-58 http://www.hemingwayapp.com

INDEX

ABOUT A BOOK APART

We cover the emerging and essential topics in web design and development with style, clarity, and above all, brevity—because working designer-developers can't afford to waste time.

COLOPHON

The text is set in FF Yoga and its companion, FF Yoga Sans, both by Xavier Dupré. Headlines and cover are set in Titling Gothic by David Berlow.

This book was printed in the United States using FSC certified Finch papers.